ONLY IN
LOUISIANA

A Guide for the Adventurous Traveler

The tomb of a pipe fitter. Main Street Cemetery, Plaquemine

ONLY IN LOUISIANA

A Guide for the Adventurous Traveler

by

KEITH ODOM

QUAIL RIDGE PRESS

Baton Rouge / Brandon

Library of Congress Cataloging-in-Publication Date

Odom, Keith.
    Only in Louisiana: a guide for the adventurous traveler/by
Keith Odom.
        p. cm.
    Includes index.
    ISBN 0-937552-56-9 : $6.95
    1. Louisiana--Guidebooks. 2. Louisana--Miscellanea.
3. Curiosities and wonders--Louisiana--Guidebooks. I. Title.
F367.3.036 1994
917.6304'63--dc20   94-36015
                                                          CIP

QUAIL RIDGE PRESS
P.O. Box 123 · Brandon, MS 39043
1-800-343-1583

Photos by Keith Odom, unless otherwise noted
Designed by Barney McKee

CONTENTS

LAGNIAPPE 115

MAP OF LOUISIANA
with approximate site locations

PREFACE

Years ago, I spoiled a college bowl championship for my team by missing the question, "What is the highest point in Louisiana?" That mistake haunted me and haunted me until one day I decided to confront my shame and conquer Driskill Mountain. When I finally stood beside that hand-painted marker, at 535 feet above sea level, I felt that I'd not only redeemed myself, but succeeded in a quest.

Only in Louisiana is the chronicle of a series of quests. With notepad and camera in hand, I have tried to seek out the liveliest festivals, most original craftspeople, most intriguing historical landmarks, and tastiest restaurants Louisiana has to offer. The journeys to and from have been just as exhilarating as the destinations. I've visited towns that I never knew existed, or that I knew only as tiny dots on a map. Our state is full of secrets, and the best way to discover them is to venture down old highways and small country roads. Who knows when you'll come upon a wildlife garden, or a unique country restaurant, or a festive carnival, or a picturesque cemetery tucked beneath moss-draped trees?

Louisiana is a large state and no doubt I've missed a few things that might have been included. I haven't tried to give exhaustive coverage to any of the categories I present, most of which could support books of their own. New Orleans presented an astounding array of possibilities, but most are already well known and have been written about; I chose only a few that I thought would provide an interesting sampling of these possibilities. My selections are highly subjective, and represent people, places, and events that showed me a unique side of Louisiana.

A few tips for travelers. Private individuals listed here welcome visitors, but it's best to call before you drop by. Festival dates vary slightly from year to year, so consult local chambers of commerce or tourist bureaus for exact dates. Call restaurants ahead (especially if you're driving from a long way) to confirm hours.

I hope you'll enjoy the quest for the unique side of Louisiana as much as I have. If you find other exciting people, places, and events that you think would be suitable for future editions, I would certainly be interested in hearing about them. Drop me a line at P. O. Box 83662, Baton Rouge, LA 70884, or call 1-800-343-1543.

K. O.
September, 1994

ACKNOWLEDGMENTS

Special thanks to Lorraine Redd, author of *Only in Mississippi*, for her inspiring example; to Gwen and Barney McKee and the QRP staff for their editorial assistance and encouragement; to Janet Odom, Jan Albert, and Hal Odom for their cameras and editorial eyes; to Laurie Ransome, David Hendry, Mike Korn, and Mark Bahm for their valuable input; and to Lester Adams, Carola Ann Andrepont, Frances Doga, Lois Dugas, Wayne Fulmer, Dixie Gaspard, Rodney Guilbeaux, Margo Hicks, Tina Landry, Jeanette Martinez, Bob Powers, Sherry Romero, Chris Thayer, Preston Verret, Sandra Wells, Michael Wynne, and my office colleagues for suggestions and support.

Peckerwood Hill Store near Winnfield

The "goat tree"

Artists, Craftspeople

JEWELS OF THE HORN
West Monroe

Don't be surprised if you hear a loud horn blast the next time you're in West Monroe. It's probably Nalda Gilmore or one of his daughters testing the latest creation of Jewels of the Horn.

Forty-five years ago, Nalda Gilmore learned the art of making hunting horns out of bulls' horns from fellow West Monroe resident V. A. Capers. When Mr. Capers passed away, Mr. Gilmore was virtually the last practitioner of this art—that is, until his daughters Olivia Gates and Nelda Rowlan took an interest. They proved such astute apprentices that now they're enjoying a "horn of plenty," and Nalda's art will surely live on.

What exactly *is* a hunting horn? It's a musical instrument played like a trumpet or bugle that was used long ago to summon workers from the fields at mealtime. Hunting clubs use them nowadays to communicate with other hunting clubs in the woods and to call dogs. Jewels of the Horn horns are prized for their distinctive timbre and their range of audibility. Nalda says a blow on one of his horns can carry up to three miles in good conditions. After hearing Nalda, Nelda, and Olivia demonstrate, I'm inclined to agree!

In the showroom, you can see hunting horns of an astonishing variety. Each instrument has its own shape, grain, striping, and pitch. Goat and ram horns are used as well as cow horns. The family sells most of its ram horns to synagogues, where they are used as *shophars*.

Cow horns are imported in crates by the thousands from the Watusi

Nalda Gilmore

tribe in Africa. They arrive "green" and have to be dried for a full year before they can be worked. Dried horns are polished using a homemade sanding machine with three different sanding belts. The solid tip is sawed off; it is later routed out and fashioned into a mouthpiece. The open end is cropped to whatever length necessary to produce the desired pitch.

Goat and ram horns come from domestic suppliers. Goat horns take a particularly long time to dry; to speed up the process, the skulls are nailed to a tree. Be sure to ask Nalda or Olivia or Nelda to show you the "goat tree."

All shop equipment is made from salvaged parts of other machines. No part of any horn is wasted; splinters and scraps are worked into jewelry, and dust from the sanding process is collected and used as compost.

The family makes not only hunting horns and jewelry, but an assortment of Indian crafts which they show at pow-wows and conferences. Nelda is an accomplished painter who paints Indian designs on cow skulls. She and Olivia also make turtle shell rattles, camel bone necklaces, ceremonial fans, powder horns, and other crafts. They also do scrimshaw.

On weekdays, you can view and purchase Jewels of the Horn's creations under a canopy at 113 Downing Pines Road in West Monroe. Prices are surprisingly reasonable. If you'd like a demonstration of this fascinating art, call (318) 388-1638 a few days ahead of time.

Olivia Gates

SWAMP IVORY CREATIONS

Abbeville

They come from the jaws of carnivorous reptiles. They're worn by TV and movie stars. They look like ivory, but they're not. What are they?

Swamp Ivory Creations! We don't have elephants in Louisiana, but we have alligators, and Kathy Richard of Abbeville has perfected the art of working alligator teeth into exotic jewelry. Earrings, pins, and pendants of infinite variety—all made from teeth that might have ripped a tortoise shell in half!

Kathy Richard didn't start out as a jeweler; she started out as a photographer. Her life changed when a party of alligator hunters invited her to take photographs of one of their expeditions. When they set out, they were afraid they wouldn't catch very much; as it happened, they caught far more than usual, and Kathy was proclaimed a good luck charm. The hunters presented her with one of the heads as a trophy.

With the teeth from that first head, she made gift items for her friends at the University of Southwestern Louisiana in Lafayette. The designs stirred so much interest that she started making alligator tooth jewelry in earnest. Now, she has to buy about 500 heads a year to keep up with the demand.

When she obtains a fresh head from a hunter or skinner, she must first cut out the tongue and dispose of it: the tongue is very fleshy and can emit a foul odor as it decomposes. She puts the head in an outdoor fenced-in area to dry until the teeth are almost ready to fall out. Then she places it on a tin sheet that catches the teeth.

Kathy Richard

Each tooth is polished six separate times. Kathy's technique is her "secret recipe." She does her work in a former slaughterhouse that was converted to a studio in the early '60s (you can still see horn marks on the wood). She has work areas for polishing, buffing, and metalworking. Each design is unique and copyrighted.

The wall of her studio is covered with photos of Kathy selling jewelry to John Goodman, Rita Coolidge, Dyan Cannon, Phylicia Rashad, and other celebrities. Kathy's art was recently the subject of a *Ripley's Believe It or Not* column.

Kathy emphasizes that the green alligator heads she uses are obtained in full compliance with state conservation laws, and that her activities do not place the alligator population in danger.

If you go to Swamp Ivory Creations, be sure to pay a visit to Kathy's husband, John. He makes saddles by hand and is quite a craftsman. The Richards have a '40s-era cattle auction arena on their property which they're converting into a theatre for concerts and plays relating to the Cajun experience. Be on the lookout for exciting events there in the future.

Swamp Ivory Creations is located at 1307 S. Henry in Abbeville. Call (318) 893-5760 for more information, or drop by if you're in the area. The Richards will be happy to show you their works.

Alligator head drying pen

GOURDS, GOURDS, GOURDS!

Oak Grove

"People always tell me I'm out of my gourd," says Cora Mae Overby. But public opinion doesn't stop her from doing what she loves best: cultivating and decorating gourds. She's been practicing her craft in the northeast Louisiana town of Oak Grove for the last ten years, and her dedication shows.

Peek through the front glass of Ms. Overby's realty office on Main Street in Oak Grove (La. 2) and you'll see ornamental gourds of an astonishing diversity. Easter bunnies, Santa Clauses, baskets, dippers, jugs, wall hangings—anything your mind can conceive (and several things it can't!)—all wrought to perfection by Cora Mae Overby's artistry.

The gourd is a vine-growing vegetable closely related to the squash and the pumpkin. When ripe, it is over 90% water. Most varieties are bitter and inedible. American Indians prized gourds for their tough, wood-like exterior and their utility as containers. Ms. Overby came to appreciate them as a child during the Great Depression, when her family was forced to relocate several times: household articles that were inexpensive, lightweight, and durable were kept rather than discarded.

After numerous moves, Ms. Overby finally settled in Oak Grove in 1952. Now, with her own patch of land, she makes an extensive

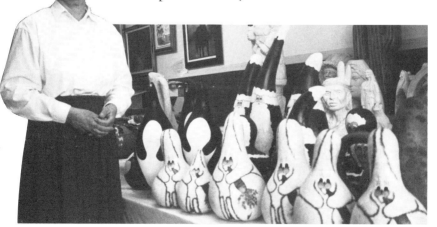

Cora Mae Overby

planting of gourd vines every February, usually on trellises. By August, she's ready to harvest. Gourds are picked when their stems, or *curls,* are dead. Due to their high water content, gourds must be dried for a year before they can be worked. Ms. Overby places hers on special mats to prevent them from spoiling.

She then hollows them out and applies primer to their wood-like surfaces. At this stage of the process, she allows her artistic spirit to take over. Who knows what she'll make? Be it a rabbit, a duck, or a water pitcher, she sketches and paints the design freehand, allows it to dry, then sprays the exterior with acrylic sealer. Mrs. Overby is a painter as well as a gourd artist; she has sold many of her landscapes at shows in Louisiana and neighboring states.

One of Ms. Overby's favorite uses for gourds is to make purple martin houses. She dearly loves the mosquito-eating birds, and believes they feel more comfortable in dwellings made of all-natural material. She carves small circular holes in the sides of whitewashed gourds, then hangs them on tall, metal hangers that resemble umbrellas with no webbing. All her neighbors own these umbrella-rib purple martin condominiums, and in springtime, all units are occupied!

"I don't know what it is about gourds, they're just fascinating," says Ms. Overby. "I love to watch them grow, see the different shapes. Gourd is good therapy." Drop by Oak Grove Realty and I think you'll agree.

To get to Ms. Overby's shop, take La. 165 north from Monroe. La. 165 changes into La. 2. Follow La. 2 into Oak Grove (about one hour) and look for Oak Grove Realty on the south side of the street just before the courthouse. Call (318) 428-9452 for further information.

Umbrella-rib purple martin house

SHELL ART BY MICKEY

Constance Beach

Mickey Guilbeaux has walked the beaches of Cameron Parish every day for the last 18 years gathering seashells. She averages five miles a day. Five miles a day x 365 days a year x 18 years = over 32,000 miles, or 1¼ times the circumference of the earth! When she says that Constance Beach, a community 19 miles east of the Texas border, has a greater variety of shells than anywhere else on the Louisiana coast, I believe her.

Ask Mickey to show you her "raw" shells. Overflowing crates of whelks and conchs on her back porch suggest that her tireless walking pays off. Before selling them, she submerges them in a solution of one part muriatic acid to three parts water for eight seconds, then coats them with acrylic. This process elicits astonishing hues, all of them natural. Mickey never paints any of her shells; she'd rather let nature speak for itself.

Inside her shop, you can see gallon buckets of the smaller varieties—wintle traps, cateyes, olives, docinas, periwinkles—all

Mickey and Rodney Guilbeaux

cleaned, categorized, and ready to be hot-glued into shell creations. One of her most popular items is an oval-shaped mirror with shells around the border. Another is a cross made of gar scales. Gar scales have very sharp edges and were once used as arrowheads by Indians. She also does a brisk business in shell-art ducks, pigs, pelicans, night lights, wind chimes, candy dishes, various types of jewelry—even human figures!

For gamblers, she carries sea beans of all sizes. Superstition has it that if you carry a sea bean in your pocket, you'll have good luck at the gaming tables. (I wonder if it would help with lottery numbers....) Be sure to pick up a "Crucifix Bone," the head bone of a saltwater catfish that looks just like Jesus on the cross.

Shell Art By Mickey doubles as a notary office. Mickey's husband, Rodney, is a Cajun joketeller, notary public, and active member of 19 civic organizations. He is an expert on coastal erosion and frequently speaks to schools and other groups. Mickey stays busy too: she takes exhibits of shells to schools and gives shell tours to busloads of schoolchildren at the shop. Both she and Rodney know a lot about life in the southwest corner of the state, and are well-informed about nearby tourist attractions.

Constance Beach has that rarest of commodities on the Louisiana coast, a white sandy beach. The ambiance of the community is tranquil and safe. Don't overlook this peaceful spot on your next trip, and be sure to visit the lady who sells seashells by the seashore.

To get to Shell Art By Mickey, take the Sulphur exit from I-10 (La. 27), and head south. When you reach the Gulf of Mexico (La. 82), take a right. About five miles later, take a left on Cameron Road 517, then a fast right on Cameron Road 521. For further information, call (318) 569-2159.

RAYMOND SEDOTAL

Pierre Part

To look at one of Raymond Sedotal's freshly-carved pintail ducks, you'd never believe he'd only been carving for three years. I didn't. Until I ran my fingers along a pintail decoy's back, I thought he'd stolen feathers from a real pintail and glued them on.

Detail is what sets Mr. Sedotal apart from scores of other wood carvers in South Louisiana's swamps and bayous, *detail* an order of magnitude sharper than the closest competition. Each carving requires at least 200 hours of his concentration, and the labor shows. He has won accolades at many statewide expositions, and recently took fourth place in a nationwide competition in Baltimore.

A typical duck carving begins as a rectangular block of tupelo gum (a soft, light wood used to make packing crates and broom handles, among other things). Mr. Sedotal sketches an overhead view of the duck on the top of the block, a bottom view on the bottom, and so on for all the sides. He cuts around each outline with a band saw, leaving about a finger's width of spare wood.

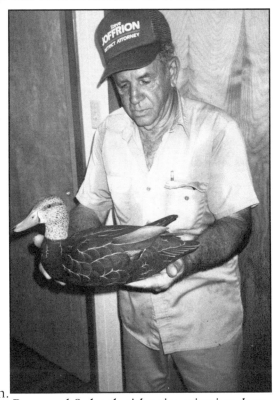

Fine details are later delineated with a knife. The entire duck is carved from a single block of wood: nothing artificial is added except the eyes, which come from a special mail order supply house.

Once the carving is complete, he "burns" the wood. Burning consists of passing the wood lightly through a flame in order to seal the moisture in and prime the surface for paint. The first layer of paint is usually brown.

Raymond Sedotal with prize-winning decoy

On top of the brown base, he adds bands of violet, green, and blue, then covers the whole with black. With this technique, he is able to capture the opalescent sheen of a live duck's feathers. Hold one of Mr. Sedotal's wood ducks up to the light and rotate it slightly. You'll see faint shades of purple and blue shining through the black.

Mr. Sedotal doesn't restrict himself to ducks. He carves eagles, geese, red-winged blackbirds, and other flying creatures as well. One of his most sought-after creations is a cypress oar with an engraving of a duck at the bottom. He also gathers cypress knees (the part of a cypress tree's root system that grows above water) and steams them. Polished and mounted, cypress knees look like ivory-colored stalagmites.

That Mr. Sedotal should be such a talented wood carver comes as no surprise to his neighbors in Pierre Part. His family has been building cypress pirogues for three generations. Despite the recent popularity of aluminum boats, Mr. Sedotal continues to make high-quality cypress boats that continue to be in demand. He teaches a well-attended course in boat building at Nicholls State University in Thibodaux. He also makes miniature pirogues, one of which is on display at the Folk Life Center in the basement of the State Capitol in Baton Rouge.

Why does Mr. Sedotal carve? *"C'est tranquille,"* he says, meaning "It's peaceful" in Cajun French. Mr. Sedotal still speaks Cajun French as comfortably as English. But carving is also profitable. A pair of wood ducks might net him $1,500. He attends festivals throughout Louisiana and other states, and often sells everything he brings.

But he's still willing to exhibit his wares to lovers of fine carving. If you plan to be in Pierre Part, call him in advance at (504) 252-6322. To get to Pierre Part, take the Donaldsonville exit from I-10. Take La. 70 to the Sunshine Bridge (warning: $1.00 toll). Follow La. 70 to Pierre Part.

MAE SOUDELIER

Houma

"I recycle everything!" She says it, and she means it. Whenever artist Mae Soudelier sees something somebody else is about to throw away, her mind clicks—and voilà, a new creation!

Old pickle jars, water jugs, curtains, bedspreads, clothing material, rope, pine cones, corn shucks, fish scales, turtle shells—these are Mae Soudelier's canvases and oils. With them she creates a variety of decorative items that defy easy categorization. One of her favorites is a mosaic-style portrait of an African dancer, with seed pods from a pine cone for hair and a chicken bone for an earring. By her doorway is a large pickle jar, painted light blue, with a picture of the Blessed Virgin Mary ringed by a rosary. "But I had to buy the rosary," she admits.

Friends and family often give her scraps of material to make pictures with. The day I visited, she had just created a floral fabric design out of an old bedspread and some discarded curtain material. The detail of the flowers was so intricate that I asked her if the flowers were already printed on the curtain. "No indeed!" she said. "I cut those out with tiny little scissors!"

The most startling creation at Ms. Soudelier's home is a wall planter made out of a giant loggerhead turtle shell. Measuring two feet from top to bottom, it dominates the decor of the back porch. She found the dead turtle in a roadway, scooped out its insides, and set the shell on an anthill. The ants scavenged the shell clean. Then she scrubbed it with bleach, waxed it, outlined the scales with a black marker, and a planter was born.

Every wall and flat surface in Mae Soudelier's house is adorned with one of her recycled ornamental creations.

Loggerhead turtle shell planter

A very nice model of a magnolia blossom, made from tarpon fish scales, leans against the doorjamb to her bedroom. She often has to sell her wares at local festivals to make extra room. From start to finish, a wall hanging takes her only 12 hours, so her house does get crowded! (Don't worry—she photographs everything before she sells it.) Her sense of thrift was cultivated during the Depression, when "If you had one dollar, you had to make it do for two."

Ms. Soudelier ("Mama Mae," as she's known to friends) is happy to exhibit her creations. She is also a poet, a philosopher, and a lively conversationalist. Call her at (504) 876-2932 to make an appointment.

"Mama Mae" with one of her creations

NEUBIG ART GALLERY
Baton Rouge

"A bomb could go off and nobody could disturb him," says Linda Neubig of husband Henry's concentration. Prolific, professional, and fabulously frugal, Henry Neubig has earned national acclaim for his haunting Louisiana scenes, all painted with the most plentiful medium imaginable—Louisiana mud. The only other ingredient he uses is Louisiana egg yolk, which serves as a fixator.

His scenes are familiar but genially nostalgic: farms, Acadian dwellings, plantation homes, boat moorings, swamps, wild flowers. Natives will recognize them all. Each painting is realized in vibrant hues that reflect Louisiana's variegated soil. "Louisiana topsoil has a greater variety of colors than Arizona topsoil, but you can't tell because everything's covered with vegetation," the Plaquemine native says.

Aeons ago, the Mississippi River built the land which is now Louisiana with alluvial deposits drained from a great North American basin bordered on the west by the Rockies and the east by the Appalachians. Thus, Louisiana is a "melting pot" of American mud.

Neubig's "oils" consist entirely of indigenous mud colors. Yellow, pink, and orange come from the Felicianas; green comes from northern parishes near the Arkansas border; black comes from Dulac, south of Houma, and is called "Dulac Black"; brown comes from near Bunkie, and is called "Bunkie Brown." Friends and relatives bring him mud samples from their hunting and hiking trips around the state. "But nobody's ever found blue mud," he says.

Art lovers in other states bring him mud "by the trunkload." Neubig has a connoisseur's appreciation for mud and never turns it away, but he refrains from using it in his work. True to his convictions, he sticks with Louisiana mud. He saves small quantities of donated mud in buckets for his "mud collection."

The versatile Neubig often has five to six paintings in progress simultaneously. This is partly because the wet sections of a painting must dry before he can paint new sections, but also because of Neubig's monumental self-discipline. In 25 years as an artist, he has never missed a deadline, a feat all the more amazing considering he does his own framing. His experience has prepared him to act swiftly on his inspirations.

When you arrive at Neubig Art Gallery, the first thing you see is the Neubigs' largest creation: their house. Henry and Linda built it from the ground up with their own hands. The stucco work took six months; Henry's signature appears on the last square. The Neubigs create whatever they can by hand, and purchase hand-made articles by other artists. They encourage all people to utilize their creative abilities.

"I've always wanted to paint dirty pictures," Henry is often quoted as saying. The opportunity to see these "dirty pictures" first-hand and talk to the artist is well worth a trip to south Baton Rouge. To get to Neubig Art Gallery, take I-12 east from downtown Baton Rouge to O'Neal Lane (Exit 7). Turn right at the bottom of the ramp and go one mile to Strain Road. Take a right on Strain Road and follow it ½ mile down to 16950, which is on the right. For information, call (504) 275-5126.

Courtesy Artists of Louisiana & Arkansas

Henry Neubig with mud painting

Restaurants

BORDELON'S
French Settlement

A ferry yoke cemented to the front of Bordelon's Restaurant in French Settlement reminds diners that this site was once the end of the line for overland travel in Livingston Parish. La. 16 came to a dead stop at the Amite River, and the only way to get to Ascension Parish was to ride the ferry.

Travelers still stop at the Old Ferry Landing, but now for a different reason: to partake of Chef Jay Root's cuisine. From Baton Rouge, New Orleans, and as far away as Scandinavia they come, and none leave disappointed.

In 1902, the building which would later become Bordelon's was constructed as an ice house. Great blocks of ice covered with sawdust were hauled up from New Orleans on barges and stored there. The building was remodeled and operated as the Mecca Inn and the Rebel Inn before Jay Root took over. If you look closely at the Bordelon's sign, you can see the old Rebel Inn sign underneath.

Bordelon's overlooks the Amite River. Fishing camps line the Livingston Parish side, but the opposite bank is a game preserve which will never be developed. The ambience is exotic; alligators and herons are common sights. Make it a point to arrive early enough to watch the sun set over the water. Stroll out to the "After Deck," an outdoor area where live bands often play, and take a drink from the artesian well that flows from the side of a tree whenever the Mississippi River is high enough.

Jay Root has worked around food all his life, starting out as an apprentice at the Holiday Inn in Hammond. He opened a succession of nightclubs in Baton Rouge and Lafayette before opening Jay's Le Bistro in New Orleans in 1985. He's studied under Kay Prudhomme (wife of Chef Paul Prudhomme) and Chef John Folse (of Lafitte's Landing). Original creations like Steak Henley, Grilled Pork Maurepas, and Trout on Spinach have won blue ribbons for Jay, a considerable feat in gastronomically competitive South Louisiana. Among his other favorites are Orange Roughy with Shrimp Sauce and Baby Veal with Sautéed Mushrooms.

Dynamic Jay makes daily runs to the Louisiana coast to buy seafood—that is, after rising at 5:30 a.m., making a few sauces and salads, and warming up the kitchen for his crew. At dinnertime he's always on the premises, keeping an eye on the kitchen and stopping at tables to make sure everything is just right. He's contemplating renaming the restaurant "Rouxt's," a name which reflects his Creole cooking background and his personal dedication to the restaurant.

How does Jay succeed? "It has to come from here," he says, pointing to his heart. "You have to love the business and be willing to make the sacrifices." Make the drive to Bordelon's and I think you'll agree his heart is in the right place.

To get to Bordelon's, take I-10 to exit 22 and go north. Take a left at La. 16 and follow the signs. For information and reservations, call (504) 698-3804 or (504) 695-6903.

Bordelon's

FREEMAN & HARRIS CAFÉ

Shreveport

Folks, if you eat for comfort, this is the place for you. Freeman & Harris Café has been serving up the best southern-style cooking in North Louisiana since 1921, and nearly all those cars you see circling the parking lot and blocking the street at lunchtime are repeat customers.

What keeps the regulars coming back are the lunch specials. Typical main courses include chicken and dumplings, smothered pork chops, fried catfish, and meat loaf, all served with two vegetables, cornbread, and rice or mashed potatoes. Iced tea (sweetened unless you specifically ask otherwise) comes in giant glasses that are frequently refilled. Serving sizes are large and prices are low, like they've always been.

Venturing from the tried-and-true lunch specials, you'll discover the menu has surprising depth: fried livers, fried gizzards, smothered giblets, frog legs, and stuffed shrimp, to give a few examples. Save room—hard as that may be—for a slice of pie after lunch. The Freeman & Harris concept of a "slice" equates to roughly one-fourth of a pie. You may not finish it, but make the effort. I've eaten pies and I've eaten pies, but none can top Freeman & Harris's.

As if the food isn't enough, what makes Freeman & Harris Café special is that it's been continuously owned and operated by African-Americans Van Freeman and Jack Harris since it opened its doors in 1921. Some sources believe it is the oldest black-owned eating establishment in the United States. Although the restaurant's proprietorship has been disputed in recent years, the quality of service has never declined. Many employees have worked there for decades.

Even more to its credit is that the restaurant has never witnessed race-related violence, not even during the racially-turbulent '60s. Lunchtime crowds are always a mixture of black and white customers. Quality food, low prices, and attentive service have enabled this establishment to achieve what so many government programs have not: racial harmony.

Though you'll have plenty of food to occupy your thoughts, don't forget to look around at the decor. Original paintings of Louisiana scenes by Louisiana artists adorn every panel of every wall. There's also a well-stocked jukebox. Celebrities such as Stevie Wonder, Sugar Ray Robinson, and Gladys Knight have made special detours to visit Freeman & Harris's while in the area.

Freeman & Harris Café is located at 317 Pete Harris Drive (formerly Western Avenue). Exit I-20 at Market Street and follow the direction of the ramp. At Texas Street, turn left. Go to the end of Texas Street and turn right onto Common Street. Go two blocks and turn left on Caddo Street. Take the left fork in the road onto Pete Harris Drive (Western). The restaurant is about one block from the fork. Call (318) 425-7786 for further information.

Freeman & Harris Café

JOE'S DREYFUS STORE RESTAURANT

Livonia

Don't expect to eat everything on your plate at Joe's Dreyfus Store. Even if you're a big eater, you'll probably need a takeout box. That's all part of the reputation Joe Majors has established for the Livonia restaurant he opened in 1989.

Joe is no newcomer to cooking. He began honing his considerable culinary skills in the '60s at Piccadilly Cafeteria in Baton Rouge, and has worked for or owned at least ten establishments since, including prestigious restaurants in New Orleans, Atlanta, and Phoenix. He ran the acclaimed Red Barn Café in Livonia before moving to his present location.

The building that houses Joe's Dreyfus Store Restaurant has a story of its own. It was used for years as Livonia's general store. Acquired by a German immigrant named Theodore Dreyfus in 1902, it was remodeled in 1925 into roughly its present configuration and was managed by family members until 1988. When they retired, Joe moved in. One of his goals in opening the restaurant was to preserve the general store's social focus as a place for friends to meet and converse in a relaxed setting.

Joe's Dreyfus Store Restaurant

Conversations I've overheard while waiting for a table often center around food, particularly the sumptuous fare they've eaten in the past or would like to eat at Joe's Dreyfus Store. Perhaps the most talked-about entrée is Catfish Breaux Bridge, an entire (not fileted) catfish smothered with crawfish étouffée and accompanied by a full complement of vegetables. The catfish overlaps the edge of the plate, and the portion of étouffée is large enough to make a meal in itself. Another celebrated dish is quail stuffed with oyster dressing. *Stuffed* is the operative word here.

Seafood is emphasized on the menu, but other dishes hold their own. Pork tenderloin is a good example. The lean pork loin served over red cabbage with smothered potatoes will satisfy a craving for German food. Also available are boudin, fried chicken, frog legs, a variety of sandwiches, and any type of salad imaginable.

Lovers of sweets will be pleased to know that the dessert menu is no mere afterthought. A house favorite is Red Barn Crunch, which consists of rich vanilla ice cream rolled in pecans, butter brickle, and chocolate. Not on the printed menu but well worth asking for is the coffee custard. Its silky texture and subtle taste could tempt a saint.

While waiting for your meal, be sure to notice the decor. Framed advertisements from the '20s share the walls with old farming tools and other general store merchandise. A glass case along one wall displays antique apothecary items and toys. The bare wood floor calls to mind the building's general store past.

Joe Majors has worked at many restaurants in many cities. The long lines you see every day at Joe's Dreyfus Store in Livonia are eloquent testimony that he's found his niche. Make the drive and I think you'll agree.

The most direct route to Joe's Dreyfus Store is to take U.S. 190 to La. 77 (about 30 miles from Baton Rouge). Turn left on La. 77 and look for the big white building about a block down on the right. For a more scenic route, take I-10 to the Ramah/ Maringouin exit (La. 3000) and head north. Stay on the same road as it changes to La. 76 and La. 77. The restaurant will be on the left in approximately 12 miles. Along this meandering road, you can see splendid live oaks, bayous, and farm scenes.

For more information, call (504) 637-2625.

FLEUR-DE-LIS COCKTAIL LOUNGE

Baton Rouge

Art deco pink and neon bright, the Fleur-de-Lis Cocktail Lounge in Baton Rouge is unique and distinctive. Little has changed here since Mama and Papa Guercio introduced "Roman Pizza Pie" to a skeptical public in the late '40s. That includes a steady clientele, a tried-and-true menu, and service that makes all comers feel like family.

No one knows exactly when the original building was built. Through the '20s, it was used as a gas station/grocery store. After the repeal of prohibition, it was converted to a cocktail lounge, and the name was changed to Fleur-de-Lis. The familiar pink front and neon lighting were probably added during the '30s. "Mama" Annie and "Papa" Joe Guercio bought the business in 1946.

One day in 1949, Mama Guercio decided to try an informal market survey. She had discovered an old-world recipe for Italian

Fleur-de-Lis Cocktail Lounge with trademark Jax Beer sign

pizza pie, and handed out free slices of it to her bar customers. The response was less than enthusiastic. Anchovy pizza and beer just didn't seem to go together. But she stuck with her idea, making minor modifications in the recipe, until she hit upon a combination of ingredients her customers liked. They acquired such a craving for the new dish that she had to invest in new pizza pans. Unable to purchase circular pizza pans, she settled for rectangular cookie sheets. Fleur-de-Lis pizza has been rectangular ever since.

As late as the early '50s, "service cabins" were attached to both sides of the restaurant. Employees lived in these cabins. Jo Smith was born and raised in one, and still works at the restaurant today. She recalls when Government Street was nothing but a gravel road leading into wilderness. The vintage Jax Beer sign on the front of the building has been there as long as she can remember, as has the indoor wooden phone booth (though the telephone is up-to-date).

A great hallmark of the Fleur-de-Lis is continuity. Annie Polk has worked in the kitchen for 25 years and has no intention of quitting. The menu is simple but solid: pizza. The two most popular combinations are Round-the-World and Banana Pepper with Italian Sausage. All dough, sauce, and Italian sausage are made from scratch. For most customers, the only decision to make is whether or not to have anchovies.

Conventional wisdom has it that more political deals have been cut behind the walls of the Fleur-de-Lis than in the state capitol. Frequent sightings of state legislators would seem to bear this out. Celebrities also appear from time to time. During the filming of *Everybody's All-American* in 1987, Dennis Quaid and Timothy Hutton paid many visits.

The atmosphere of the Fleur-de-Lis is neighborly. Regulars bring children and grandchildren, ensuring that old traditions will survive. Despite its ties to the past, Fleur-de-Lis is definitely a restaurant with a future. It succeeds because it dares not to give in to change.

Fleur-de-Lis is located at 5655 Government Street. Locals can generally direct you to it, but you can find it by exiting I-10 at Acadian Thruway, traveling north to Government Street, and turning right on Government Street. Phone-in orders are accepted. Call (504) 924-2904 for more information.

LEA'S LUNCHROOM
Lecompte

Before interstates 10 and 49 were built, the fastest way to get to Shreveport from Baton Rouge or New Orleans was to take U.S. 71. The names of towns along the way are etched into the memories of motorists who drove that ancestral route: Bunkie, Cheneyville, Meeker, Lecompte.

Lecompte (pronounced la-COUNT) made a perfect half-way stopping point, and the perfect place to stop in Lecompte was Lea's Lunchroom. It beckoned from the wide median strip of U.S. 71 with its huge block-letter sign, whitewashed front, and untarnished reputation for satisfying customers. Jovial Mr. Lea (Lea Johnson), who established the restaurant in 1928, frequently circulated among the tables at noontime making sure things were running smoothly.

Traffic along the old highway has diminished, but the faithful keep coming back. No one objects to the short detour for Lea's bounteous plate lunches, splendid pies, and strong coffee. No one objects to the prompt service, either. Waiters greet you at the door with the question, "Lunch, sandwich, or pie?" Printed menus exist, but the smart way to go is to order a plate lunch. Your waiter can recite the day's offerings from memory. Lunches typically include ham, red beans and rice, two vegetables, and cornbread. Your plate arrives so quickly you barely have time to taste your ice water. If you're not ravenously hungry, a sandwich will suffice. Coca Cola is served in icy 6½-ounce bottles.

Save room if at all possible for dessert. Lea's pie is legendary in Central Louisiana. My favorite is cherry, but the apple, pecan, and cream varieties are all superb. Many customers come in mid-morning or mid-afternoon just for pie and coffee. You can also buy whole pies.

Another specialty is baked hams. For years, our family enjoyed a Lea's baked ham at Christmastime, and it became one of the high points of the season. I'm convinced no other ham could surpass it.

A wood-engraved motto posted on the north wall of the restaurant reads: "He who enters here is a stranger but once." My interpretation: "He who enters Lea's once will enter again." The restaurant is a short 2.4 miles from I-49, and it's still a great place to recharge your batteries. It was voted best place to get a po-boy or sandwich in Central Louisiana in a recent *Louisiana Life* reader survey.

To get there, exit I-49 at La. 112 and go east about 7 miles. La. 112 intersects with U.S. 71, and Lea's is situated between the northbound and southbound lanes of U.S. 71 at the highway crossing.

La. 112 is noteworthy in itself. I counted *at least* 36 nurseries between I-49 and U.S. 71. The panorama of all the sprinklers and neatly regimented fields is quite remarkable. Forest Hill, a nearby community, holds a nursery festival every year.

Lea's Lunchroom

MIDWAY GROCERY

Grosse Tête

Midway Grocery has been selling the necessities of life to folks in Grosse Tête since 1903. When the floor squeaks under your feet and sunlight slips in through the cracks in the bare cypress planks, you won't have to be told that you've entered a vintage turn-of-the-century Louisiana building. Forties-era posters of Royal Crown Cola and other products add to the genial, nostalgic atmosphere of this country store.

Richard Glaser has managed Midway Grocery since graduating from college in 1991. His parents, Charles and Genevieve Glaser, are the owners. As a family, they are determined to maintain the store's character and quality of service. No structural changes have been made to the building since 1903. The same general-purpose selection of merchandise is on the shelves, from coffee and baking soda to sardines and sterno. The Glasers' only innovation—but a very welcome one—is the addition of a lunch counter, which serves plate lunches and short-order items.

Go in at lunchtime, and you'll see farm workers, office work-

Midway Grocery

Richard and Genevieve Glaser

ers, young folks and old folks lined up to buy take-out platters of crawfish stew over rice, smothered okra, pork roast, chicken 'n' dumplings, chili, fried catfish, vegetables, and desserts, all made each day by the Glasers' kitchen. Portions are generous and prices reasonable, so many customers never miss a day. Richard emphasizes that all his crawfish come from Louisiana, not over-seas! If you can take a leisurely lunch break, have a seat at one of the wooden tables and order one of Midway's cheeseburgers. You'll wonder how fast food ever got so popular. While you wait, look at the antique tobacco presses, sugar cane knives, and cast-iron logging tongs nonchalantly wedged between boxes of cereal and cans of soup.

National advertisers have been attracted to Midway Grocery for its down-home ambience. Chevrolet used it in a "Heartbeat of America" commercial, and A&W Root Beer did a photo layout of it for an ad in *Rolling Stone* magazine. Lovers of old-time country charm shouldn't pass this one up.

To visit Midway Grocery, take exit 139 from I-10. Go straight at the bottom of the ramp (across the bayou), and you'll see the red building about ¼ mile down on the right.

MICHAEL'S MID-CITY GRILL

New Orleans

In New Orleans, it's hard to go wrong with restaurants. Every street corner, every nook and every cranny holds out yet another fresh culinary marvel. There are 1,001 eating establishments, and at least as many excuses to toss self-control to the four winds. Of course, when you're in The Big Easy, self-control may not be your top priority.

But cost can be a problem, particularly in the French Quarter. Newcomers should be aware that many restaurants outside the French Quarter serve superb food in large portions for reasonable prices. One to which I find myself returning is Michael's Mid-City Grill. Located at Canal and North David, slightly over two miles from North Rampart Street, it is near enough to the Quarter to be reached without a gruelling drive, but far enough from the Quarter to be exempt from tourist hype and prices.

Mid-City Grill offers a well-rounded selection of soups,

Michael's Mid-City Grill

salads, and sandwiches. The black bean soup is exceptional. The spinach salad is large enough for two people, as are all the salads. Salads come with French bread slices baked with real cheese. Many heart-healthy dishes are available, such as grilled chicken and fish. A loaf of fresh French bread accompanies some entrées. Beer and mixed drinks are also served.

Regular patrons like to sit at the bar and watch TV (especially Saints games, when they're not blacked out). The floor has old-fashioned black-and-white checkerboard tile. Children and adults feel comfortable in this relaxed, neighborhood setting. Prices are quite reasonable.

Historic French Quarter establishments and trendy night spots have their place. But don't be afraid to venture beyond tourist boundaries and find the numerous excellent restaurants scattered throughout New Orleans. For a relaxing, reasonably priced meal, I'd recommend Michael's Mid-City Grill. Call (504) 486-8200 for more information.

MELVYN'S HAMBURGERS

Monroe

Walk into Melvyn's on any given night and you may see bank presidents, blue collar workers, TV anchors, Junior Leaguers, and an entire soccer team sitting side by side. Everybody in Monroe goes to Melvyn's. Where else can you get the best hamburger in the galaxy?

Melvyn's gourmet burgers are 100% pure beef, hand-made and charbroiled to your specifications, with secret flavor ingredients that possibly only one person in the world knows. They're not small, either. Most start with a one-third-pound patty and grow taller with each layer of lettuce, tomato, onion, cheese, and toppings. For a meal you'll never forget, order the Mega Burger. It's an eight-ounce patty with all the trimmings. Fresh-cut French fries accompany each sandwich. To borrow a line from a popular TV series, "This must be where hamburgers go when they die."

Health-conscious diners can order from "The Lighter Side of Melvyn's," which features the top-selling chicken teriyaki and pasta salad. Gargantuan green salads are available in many varieties. Those looking for a more lavish meal should try the 14-ounce ribeye. At $11.95, it's the most expensive item on the

Melvyn's

Melvyn's has become such an institution that it's hard to imagine a time when it wasn't there, though Melvyn McCoy assures me it opened for business in 1985. Long-time Monroe residents might recall the unlucky succession of restaurants that occupied the building before Melvyn's, including Porter's Dairy, The Huddle, Minuteman, Frank Walker's, and Brandy's. Credit is due to owners Melvyn and Diane McCoy and manager Jeff Hicks for finding a successful combination of menu and atmosphere and maintaining it.

Regular customers are greeted by name when they walk in. Many drop by daily to watch sporting events on two wide-screen TV's, chat with friends, or just relax. Alcohol is available, but the ambience is not that of a lounge. Celebrities such as Cajun musician Jo-El Sonnier and NFL quarterback Bubby Brister have sought out the restaurant on their visits to Northeast Louisiana.

Melvyn's is an excellent alternative to chain restaurants and interstate exit food. You can smell the charbroiler several blocks away, but in case you need directions: take I-20 to Civic Center Boulevard (exit 117C). Head north to Louisville Avenue. Turn right and follow Louisville to North 18th. Turn left on North 18th and follow to Forsythe. The restaurant is on the right corner just before the intersection. Call (318) 325-2055 for phone-in orders.

BOUDIN KING

Jennings

Boudin is as Cajun as crawfish, and nobody fixes boudin like Ellis Cormier. Mr. Cormier got into the restaurant business in 1975, when he decided to use the most popular item at his Jennings grocery store as the foundation of a classic Cajun restaurant. Nowadays Boudin King serves the heartiest, zestiest boudin available at a restaurant in Southwest Louisiana, and that's saying a lot.

Those of you who've never tried this delicacy will be curious to know that boudin is a highly seasoned sausage containing pork meat, pork liver, pork heart (sometimes), rice, vegetables, and seasonings, all stuffed in a sausage casing and steamed. In earlier times, boudin was made during the winter at the time of *boucherie*, or pig-butchering. Thanks to refrigeration, modern cooks can make it year round. There are as many recipes as there are cooks, and heated disputes often arise concerning how much of one ingredient or another to put in. The best cooks, like Mr. Cormier, never divulge their secrets.

But when you sit down to a few boudin links at Mr. Cormier's restaurant, the exact recipe becomes a moot point. All you have to do is enjoy. Boudin King serves both spicy and mild varieties, with mild being the recommended choice for first-time visitors. In addition to boudin, the menu offers such South Louisiana favorites as red beans and rice, chicken and sausage gumbo, fried chicken, and fried seafood, to name a few.

The ambience of Boudin King is casual and cheerful. Patrons sit at sturdy wooden tables with wooden benches and chairs. Culinary awards glimmer from the walls. Mr. Cormier considers food his highest priority—not fancy flatware and furnishings. Quality of food is also my chief concern at a restaurant; if the food is no good, I don't go back. I'll go back to Boudin King.

Incidentally, one type of boudin not available through commercial establishments is "red" or "blood" boudin. Red boudin is identical to conventional "white" boudin except that pig's blood is mixed in with the rice, pork, and seasonings. Health regulations currently prohibit the sale of red boudin, but many Cajuns still prepare it at home and consider it superior to white boudin.

The rest of the world has begun to recognize the nutritional value of Cajun cuisine. Stop at Boudin King and see just how delicious nutritious cooking can be. Take-out orders and frozen packages are available. Stock up on this South Louisiana specialty before venturing across the Sabine River.

Boudin King is located at 906 West Division Street in Jennings, which is roughly halfway between Lafayette and Lake Charles. Exit I-10 at La. 26 and go south. Cross a set of railroad tracks, then take a right on West Division Street. The restaurant is four blocks down on the right. Call (318) 824-6593 for further information.

Boudin King

Wildlife

GLOBAL WILDLIFE CENTER

Folsom

When Daisy the Giraffe sticks her head into your tram car, you *might* get nervous, especially when you realize that her head is bigger than most people's upper torsos. But you adjust. She sniffs you, eats corn from your cup, then passes to the next car.

You're at the Global Wildlife Center in Folsom, an educational park where a tour is a curious hybrid of a zoo visit and a safari. Several hundred wild animals, representing over 40 different species, roam over 900 acres of woods, grasslands, and marshes. Visitors ride in covered flatcars pulled by tractors. The tour guides know a great deal about not only animals in general but also the personalities of the individual animals. (Ask about

Daisy the Giraffe drops in for a snack.

Dreadlocks, the wily old sheep who hides whenever the shearer comes.)

Giraffes may be the largest animals at the center, but Père David Deer are the rarest. Originally found only in China, a few animals were smuggled to Europe in the 1860s by Père David, a French missionary and naturalist. A flood later annihilated the Chinese population, leaving only a handful of these deer in captivity in Europe. The Global Wildlife Center now has eight.

When you buy your tour ticket, the clerk will ask if you want to buy a cup of feed corn. Buy one. Or two. You'll be able to make friends with the animals much easier. Ubiquitous axis and black fallow deer are always eager for a treat. Bison, antelope, and Texas longhorns will eat an entire cup of corn in one gulp if you let them, but they'll also let you touch their horns (if you do it carefully!). Even ordinarily shy zebras and llamas will approach if you rattle a feed cup.

None of the animals at the center are carnivorous. You won't see lions, tigers, or bears, and you won't see elephants, rhinos, or potentially aggressive or territorial animals. The center wants to ensure the safety of both its tourists and its non-aggressive animals. And while the animals are fairly relaxed around tour groups, they are still wild and can behave unpredictably. Thus, one of Global Wildlife Center's rules is that you must stay on the tram car during the tour. (Of course, before and after the tour, feel free to pet the very fat and very content Vietnamese pot-bellied pig.)

The Global Wildlife Center is superb entertainment for children and adults alike. It's like going on a safari without having to go halfway around the world. Take I-12 to exit 47 (Robert). Go north on La. 445 for 10 miles to La. 40, then turn right. The center is one mile down on the left. For more information, call (504) 624-WILD.

Tourists enjoy feeding shy llamas.

WILDLIFE GARDENS

Gibson

If one of your ambitions is to be bitten by an alligator and live to tell the tale, James and Betty Provost's Wildlife Gardens is the place for you. Mr. Provost will happily let you stick your finger into the mouth of a five-inch baby alligator—a sensation you're not likely to forget.

The Provosts began collecting wild animals on their Terrebonne Parish property many years ago, and eventually decided to show them to the public. Virtually all South Louisiana swamp creatures are represented, some of them tame enough to be petted. You can hold a duck, pet a nutria (an aquatic rodent prized for its coat), or get within a few feet of a peacock. More fearsome creatures—wild boars, bobcats, and full-grown alligators—are safely behind fences.

Mr. Provost gives a fascinating walk-through tour of his

James Provost holds a very tame duck.

private swamp. Knowledgeable about all facets of swamp wildlife, he can tell fascinating stories about alligators, owls, and turtles, and provide a wealth of information about swamp vegetation. Don't miss the turtle pond and the "talkative alligator"! The walk-through tour also includes an authentic trapper's cabin that was used in the 1987 television movie, *Three on a Match*. The cabin contains authentic trapping tools, alligator hides, and a giant snapping turtle skull. Snapping turtles can still bite after they're dead, so watch out!

Mr. Provost is also an expert carver. Be sure to stop in the gift shop and look at his intricate tupelo carvings of ducks, crabs, and other animals. Run your finger along the edges of knives he carves from alligator jaws.

Bed and Breakfast cabins are available, as are pirogue rides. The restaurant serves snacks and Cajun cuisine.

Tours are conducted at 10:00 a.m., 1:00 p.m. and 3:30 p.m., and last about 1½ hours. Admission charged. To get to Wildlife Gardens from Houma, take U.S. 90 toward Gibson (west). Go 16 miles. Turn on the bridge at Greenwood School, and continue two miles toward Gibson. From Thibodaux or Morgan City, take U.S. 90 (east) toward Houma. At Gibson, go five miles. Turn on bridge before Cavalier's Grocery, and continue two miles toward Houma.

SWAMP MONSTER TOURS

Slidell

Riding in Roy McManus's flatboat, it's hard to imagine encountering a hostile creature in Honey Island Swamp. The scenery is exotic but tranquil. Spanish moss hangs from cypress trees that antedate the Revolutionary War; camp dwellers wave congenially as you pass; the crickets seem to be chanting a mantra.

Without a trace of effort, Captain McManus navigates swamp lanes so narrow that both sides of the boat scrape cypress trunks. A lifetime denizen of the swamp, he knows precisely what time of year the water level will and will not permit him to venture into certain areas. He turns off the engine to let passengers savor the beauty of a field of wild flowers. Then he says, "I saw a 500-pound wild boar in here once."

Local legend tells of a far more sinister inhabitant of the swamp—a hairy hominid with hunched shoulders and huge feet, a shy but dangerous creature seen only in fleeting glimpses, a mysterious "being" trapped in an evolutionary retrograde—a bigfoot. The alleged monster was first sighted 35 to 40 years ago and has reappeared intermittently since. The only tangible evidence of his existence is a plaster cast of a footprint now on display at The Pearl Gift Shoppe (the starting point for the tour). One swamp dweller several years ago called in the sheriff's department to listen to what he thought was the monster growling. To his embarrassment, the eerie sounds were found to originate from a creaky drawbridge in Slidell.

Captain McManus makes no secret of his disdain for the monster legend. "If there were a monster out there, I'd have caught it a long time ago. I'd have set my dogs on it," he says. He believes that the famous footprint was made by a 14-foot alligator that he himself killed.

Starting point of Swamp Monster tour

The Honey Island Swamp Monster was featured on an episode of the late '70s TV series, *In Search Of.* The bigfoot cognoscenti came to the conclusion that a creature of his type could conceal himself in remote areas of the swamp for a time, but would have to eat almost constantly to survive. The need for food would sooner or later drive him into contact with humans, who would get lots of chances to look at him.

Captain McManus prefers to focus on the swamp's natural beauty and on wildlife that verifiably exists. He'll speed up the boat to follow a blue heron in flight (an exhilarating experience), and throw jumbo marshmallows in the water to attract alligators. He'll point out beavers, nutria, wood ducks, snakes, hornet nests, and swamp flora. Look overhead to see some of the largest spiders in the western hemisphere.

The area has an interesting history. In the early decades of the 20th century, cypress logging was a major enterprise. Tall, straight trees were felled and towed across the Mississippi line to a sawmill. The sawmill was the largest industry in the area for many years. Recently revenue has been generated by the motion picture industry. Numerous scenes for *The Pelican Brief* were shot there. In pre-colonial days, the area was inhabited by the Acolapissa Indians. The present-day boat launch and gift shop are on old Indian land.

Mr. McManus tells jokingly of a fellow who offered to put on a bigfoot costume and make "guest appearances" for tour groups. Mr. McManus wouldn't hire him because hunters would have shot him right away. It's unlikely you'll see a monster on this tour, but you'll be enthralled by what you do see. Who knows? Old legends die hard, maybe for a reason.

Tours last two hours. Call 1-800-245-1132 to make reservations and to get directions to Indian Village. Admission charged.

Capt. Roy McManus throws marshmallows to an alligator.

Bizarre, Macabre

MYSTERY TREE
Redwing

Redwing is a small community in West Carroll Parish that didn't even make it to the Official Highway Map. Driving on Highway 2 between Oak Grove and Bastrop, you'd miss it if you weren't looking for it. And that would be a shame, because there's a sight there you have to see to believe: a cedar tree with a cherry tree growing right through the middle of it!

Oman Rutherford, lifetime resident of Bastrop, has been visiting Redwing Cemetery for many years to pay respects to

Cherry tree sprouts from cedar tree trunk

deceased relatives. One morning in 1960, he noticed a peculiar growth in the side of a cedar tree. He paid little attention to it, thinking it probably wouldn't survive. But when long branches started to grow with buds at the ends, he became curious indeed. The new growth had none of the characteristics of cedar. After several more visits to Redwing, Mr. Rutherford realized that the cedar tree had sprouted a cherry tree!

Mr. Rutherford speculates that a bird deposited a cherry seed in an exposed spot on the cedar's trunk. Deliberate grafting appears unlikely, as the cherry growth is not advantageously oriented to sunlight. And yet it thrives, weathering thunderstorms, ice storms, and insect invasions.

Over the years, the cherry tree has grown larger and hardier, possibly to the detriment of its host. The cedar is at least eight feet in circumference; Mr. Rutherford thinks it was probably planted to honor one of the cemetery's earliest residents, in about 1875. He's never heard a satisfactory explanation of how this came about—go see for yourself, and maybe you can help!

To see this mysterious dual tree, go 6½ miles west of Oakdale on La. 2. Just past the green sign that says "Redwing," you'll see an American flag on the left marking Redwing Cemetery. Turn here. The tree is in the middle of the cemetery grounds, about two-thirds of the way back from the roadway.

ST. FAUSTINE

Plattenville

Even jaded travelers will be fascinated by what they see inside Assumption Catholic Church in Plattenville. At the rear of the left aisle stands a glass sarcophagus containing a wax statue of a young girl. Look closely: her hair is real human hair.

Parishioners call the statue "St. Faustine." According to legend, the real St. Faustine lived in France many centuries ago. She spurned the amatory advances of the king, who in a fit of rage, had her beheaded. She became a symbol of purity and strength.

Father Charles Menard, pastor of St. Joseph's Church in Thibodaux, brought the statue from Rome in the mid-nineteenth century. He also brought a bone fragment from the real St. Faustine's body, which is now kept along with the statue in the glass sarcophagus. Unfortunately, the papers documenting the bone's authenticity have been lost.

From 1872 to the early 1960s, an annual procession was held in honor of St. Faustine. First her sarcophagus was polished.

St. Faustine's sarcophagus

Then the top was opened so that her hair and clothing could be brushed and her face washed. Men of the parish placed the sarcophagus on a special frame and moved it to the front of the church, where the procession would begin. Little girls dressed in white sprinkled flower petals along the procession route. Then the men hoisted the frame on their shoulders and carried it all through the church and the church grounds. Several teams were necessary because of the great weight of the case. Certain young girls, selected as "St. Faustine maids," dressed exactly like the statue and walked beside the procession.

The procession was discontinued under pressure from the Catholic Church; officials could find no historical evidence that St. Faustine really existed or that she was a saint. Still, many parishioners claim to have had prayers answered on her intervention.

Église Assomption was built on the east bank of Bayou Lafourche in 1856. The church parish has been functioning since 1793, and is one of the oldest in the state. Assumption Parish (county) was named for this church when it was carved out of Lafourche Parish in 1807. The building and grounds are magnificent in their own right.

From I-10, take La. 1 south about 35 miles. Just past Paincourtville, look for a green road sign that says "Plattenville." Turn left here. Cross the bridge over Bayou Lafourche and you'll see the church directly in front of you, on La. 308.

TRANSYLVANIA

East Carroll Parish

Transylvania. The mere name sends chills down the spines of those old enough to remember Bela Lugosi as Dracula in his most famous role.

In northeast Louisiana, there's an occidental Transylvania which bears little resemblance to its highly mythologized European counterpart. What it may lack in outright spookiness, however, it makes up for in jocularity. Ten miles south of Lake Providence in rural East Carroll Parish, Transylvania is a farming community with barely more than a post office, a gas station/gift shop, and a caution light. The strangest creatures to be found on moonlit nights are probably tourists. Still, the city has not failed to capitalize on the historical coincidence that gave it notoriety.

Norman Chappell, owner of the Transylvania General Store, believes with a fair degree of certainty that the town acquired its name when settlers from Transylvania, Kentucky, located in the area. The earliest settler was a certain Mr. Keene, whose headstone in the local cemetery gives life dates of 1805 to 1855. Thus the town was likely named in the early to mid-nineteenth century, before Bram Stoker yoked forever the names *Transylvania* and *Dracula* in the popular imagination.

Residents take a tongue-in-cheek approach to fame. A looming white water tower that greets northbound motorists on La. 65 has a huge bat and the word *Transylvania* painted in black on it. The Halloween Transylvania Festival was inaugurated in 1993 and promises to be a horror-lover's delight. The postmaster fought hard to retain the town's unique

Transylvania's "Bat Tower"

postmark; now, every fall, the office is inundated with postal patrons who want cards and packages to have Transylvania cancellations.

In 1985, employees of the general store put a cardboard box on display with this sign: "Open carefully. Baby vampire bats inside." Customers bold enough to take a peek saw two tiny plastic baseball bats inside.

A visit to this store is worth a drive up La. 65. You can buy creepy souvenirs year round, as well as hearty food and gasoline. Be sure to mail your postcards from the post office next door. You won't be able to miss the water tower. To get to Transylvania, take the La. 65 exit from I-20 and travel about 19 miles north.

VOODOO WALKING TOUR

New Orleans

One surprising fact you'll learn about voodoo is that it's not inherently evil. Like all sources of power, it can be good or bad, depending on how it's used. Looking at the macabre holdings of the New Orleans Historic Voodoo Museum (departure point for the Voodoo Walking Tour), you may be unconvinced. Human skulls, a full grown python, statues of primitive deities, totems, ritual altars, and voodoo dolls don't come off as morally neutral, at least at first. But keep an open mind.

A well-spoken guide will explain how voodoo became inextricably linked with Catholicism, dating from the era when Catholic slave owners forced their religious observances on unreceptive slaves. He'll also demystify the practice of zombification and define the original benign role voodoo dolls played in native African religion.

Leaving the museum, you'll strike out into the French Quarter, an area saturated with supernatural activity. You'll pass by an old Catholic grade school where nuns once scared children into good behavior by telling them spooky stories about a ghost who lived across the street. You'll see the house where Marie Laveau, illustrious voodoo high priestess of New Orleans, lived and raised her numerous children. You'll hear the amazing account of how

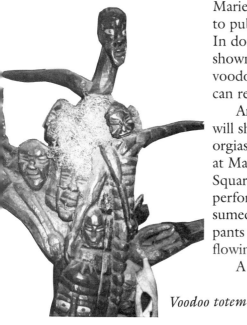

Marie Laveau singlehandedly put an end to public executions in New Orleans. In doorways and windows, you'll be shown evidence of contemporary voodoo practice that only a trained eye can recognize.

Another misconception this tour will shatter is that voodoo rituals are orgiastic. Nineteenth-century spectators at Marie Laveau's rituals in Congo Square saw other African dances being performed at the same time, and assumed that all were connected. Participants in rituals usually wear body-length flowing white garments.

A brisk walk takes you to St. Louis

Voodoo totem

Cemetery Number 1. Folks unacquainted with old New Orleans burial customs will be shocked to hear about "rental" graves and about the origin of the expression "getting the shaft." The guide tells grisly tales about the days before embalming, when above-ground tombs would crack open in the summer heat and expel noxious gases from decomposing human remains.

No doubt the highlight of the tour is the visit to Marie Laveau's tomb. The guide demonstrates the proper way to make a wish to the Voodoo Queen and gives you an opportunity to do so. He also points out the tombs of other priests and priestesses in the cemetery.

The tour concludes with a stop at the Old Pharmacy Museum. Upscale white New Orleaneans of the nineteenth century were leery of associating with voodoo practitioners, most of whom were partially or entirely black. But they still craved the power of voodoo. So they instructed pharmacists to make "potions" which they asked for by number to avoid public recognition.

Voodoo is still widely practiced today. Like New Orleans' high water table, it lies just below the topsoil of daily life. For a glimpse into this strange but alluring world, take this two-hour walking tour.

The New Orleans Voodoo Walking Tour departs from the New Orleans Historic Voodoo Museum at 724 Dumaine Street. Tours start at 1:00 p.m. daily. Price competitive with other French Quarter tours. For more information, call (504) 522-5223.

Above-ground tomb of voodoo priestess

ST. JOSEPH CEMETERY

Rayne

The first thing that strikes you about St. Joseph Cemetery in Rayne is its immaculate upkeep. Though obviously a mature cemetery, with some interments dating from the mid-1800s, it is aging gracefully. Above-ground vaults are kept glistening white, and patches of greenery between them are scrupulously clipped. The bell tower at nearby St. Joseph Catholic Church rings the Angelus in celestial tones.

Only if you're attuned to the sun, the shadows, and the time of day do you begin to feel something amiss, something you can't quite put your finger on. Suddenly it dawns on you: the vaults are oriented north-to-south instead of east-to-west. Not north-east-to-southwest or northwest-to-southeast, but *squarely* north-to-south.

Religious custom in many parts of the world holds that the deceased must be buried with their feet to the east so that they can rise to meet Christ on Judgement Day. Studies have shown that Protestants in Louisiana adhere to this practice much more rigidly than Catholics. One researcher calculated that 90% of Louisiana Protestant cemeteries followed a strict feet-to-east

St. Joseph Cemetery. Photo taken at 4:00 p.m. facing north.

Catholic cemetery on Bayou Jacob Road, Plaquemine. Vaults arranged diagonally along footpath.

orientation, while only 13% of Louisiana Catholic cemeteries did so.[1] No instances of *perpendicular* north-south orientation were found, however. Tombs in Catholic cemeteries tend to be arranged according to convenience rather than religious conviction.[2] No one in Rayne is sure what kind of "convenience" could have prompted developers to arrange the tombs as they did.

Some say it was to facilitate drainage. Personnel in the rectory at St. Joseph's say the tombs might have been deliberately positioned so as to face the front of the prior church building, which was at right angles to the present building. Others believe the original church contractors didn't have a compass. Nothing in parish records gives any clue what transpired during construction. This cemetery was once featured in *Ripley's Believe It or Not!* because of its idiosyncratic layout.

If you think you can solve the mystery, by all means drop by St. Joseph's and take a look around. Exit I-10 at La. 35 (Rayne exit—look for the frog murals) and head south. Follow La. 35 about a mile through town and you'll see the tall bell tower of St. Joseph's on the left. The churchyard is just past it.

---

[1] Tadashi Nakagawa, *The Cemetery as a Cultural Manifestation: Louisiana Necrogeography.* Doctoral Dissertation submitted to the LSU Graduate Faculty in the Department of Geography and Anthropology, May, 1987, pp. 166-170.

[2] Nakagawa, ibid.

Events

INTERNATIONAL CAJUN JOKE TELLIN' CONTEST
Opelousas

Once upon a time in South Louisiana there was a Cajun named Poo Poo Boudreaux. Ever since he was a *ti garçon* (little boy), people teased him about his name. His friends teased him, his enemies teased him, even his relatives teased him. One day he got tired of it and said, "I'm gonna go down to the courthouse and change my name *right now*."

His friend Maurice said, "Man, Boudreaux, that sounds like a good idea. What you gonna change your name to?"

"Poo Poo Arceneaux," he said.

* * *

If you're lucky enough to get a ticket to the International Cajun Joke Tellin' Contest, get ready to laugh till your ribs are sore. Each April, comedians and *raconteurs* from all over Acadiana converge on the Yambilee Building in Opelousas to show their prowess at a uniquely Louisianian art form, the Cajun joke.

What exactly *is* Cajun humor? Any Cajun can tell you—it's more than just a South Louisiana accent and a smattering of French expressions. It's an outlook, a wry but genial way of laughing at one's own foibles and life in general. It's a way of telling long stories with lots of twists and turns that are funny whether or not you remember the punchline. Cajuns never maliciously ridicule others; they invite you to laugh along with them.

Carola Ann Andrepont, originator of the annual competition and Chairman of the Opelousas Tourism & Activities Committee (OTAC), stresses the positive aspects of Cajun humor. Though

Cajun jokes can be bawdy at times, no obscene material is permitted at the competition. Contestants adhere to a strict 10-minute time limit and are rated by a panel of media personalities according to originality and authenticity to the Cajun idiom. Scores are tabulated in strictest confidentiality by a CPA firm. Eight to twelve joke tellers compete.

The winner receives the prestigious hand-carved "Poo-Yie Pelican" trophy. The pelican is the state bird of Louisiana, and "poo-yie" is an expression indicating amazement. Since many curious non-Cajuns are always in attendance, the emcee teaches the audience how (and when) to say "poo-yie" and other useful Cajun phrases.

Before the show begins, the audience is treated to a superb Cajun dinner while a live band plays. Local high school students volunteer to be servers. Trustees from nearby detention centers help set up and clean up. Ms. Andrepont says she usually has more volunteers than work for them to do.

The idea for the Cajun Joke Tellin' Competition came to Ms. Andrepont in a dream. She and other members of OTAC were brainstorming for projects to promote Opelousas. One night she went to sleep and had a vision of a competition very much like the one in existence today. Shortly thereafter, in 1988, the first competition was held.

Her dream has brought worldwide recognition to Cajun joke telling. Every year she receives phone calls from radio stations in Australia, Canada, and throughout Europe asking for sample Cajun jokes. A number of past contestants have gone on to successful careers in stand-up comedy and acting. Ms. Andrepont emphasizes that this contest is the only event in Louisiana that celebrates National Humor Month (April).

The Cajun Joke Tellin' Contest is a full evening of entertainment. Tickets go on sale in March, but don't wait to make reservations, because it's always a sell-out. Call 1-800-424-5442 for more information.

SPANISH TOWN MARDI GRAS

Baton Rouge

If America's national pastime is baseball, then Louisiana's is politics, and what better way to participate in the political process than join a Mardi Gras parade?

On the Saturday before Mardi Gras, a notorious group of revelers parades through the streets of Spanish Town, a historical district in downtown Baton Rouge, spreading a form of dementia unique to Louisiana. Floats with outrageous satirical effigies of elected officials roll by. No official is immune, from four-term Governor Edwin Edwards (a frequent target) to the lowliest alderman. Pedestrian krewes wear costumes ranging from the topical to the absurd. In 1994, one krewe dressed as carving knives to lampoon the infamous Lorena Bobbitt case.

How did this odd event begin? Some say the superheated atmosphere created by hot air from the legislature (less than a block away) drove neighborhood residents to behave in bizarre ways. Whatever the cause, the first parade rolled in 1981. Neighborhood boys improvised drums out of cardboard boxes and beat the "drums" with drumsticks while dancing down Spanish Town Road. A pickup truck with a pirogue on top was the first "float." Michael Beck, longtime Spanish Town resident and noted juggler, was the first Grand Marshall. Legend has it that Beck left the parade about halfway through to get a beer, and never came back.

In 1982, the theme was "Every Man a King." There were

Four-term Governor Edwin Edwards in one of his many Spanish Town Mardi Gras "appearances."

two pickup truck floats. Participants handed out "Beaucoup Bucks" with pictures of Edwin Edwards on them. In 1983, there were 20 floats; in recent years, there have been consistently 65 or so.

Unforgettable krewes and quasi-krewes of the past include the krewe of Yazoo, a precision lawn mower troupe who billed themselves as "The 44th Louisiana Cat Shredders" the first year; "The Universal Church of Elvis," whose members dressed in religious vestments and carried velvet icons of Elvis; and "The Sluts," a male duo who dressed in drag that would have been very convincing except for their mustaches.

Refusing to take itself too seriously is a hallmark of the parade. One 1994 float featured huge Budweiser bottles and a port-a-potty labeled "Brew Recycler." Spanish Town Mardi Gras didn't even incorporate itself until its fifth year, and its officials are determined to keep a *laissez-faire* control over it. Margo Hicks, the parade's organizer, says that absolutely no censorship is imposed on any krewe. "After all, Mardi Gras is based on a rite of spring. It's not for children," she says. Egalitarianism rules: krewes participate on a first-come, first-served basis; the King of Carnival is picked at random.

Though Spanish Town festivities have drawn over 150,000 spectators in recent years (even outdrawing LSU Tiger Football!), there's something to unnerve almost everyone. "If nobody goes home insulted, we've failed," says Margo Hicks. Never was being insulted so much fun.

Floats can sometimes get bawdy.

POKE SALAD FESTIVAL

Blanchard

Down there we have a plant that grows
   out in the woods and the fields,
Looks something like a turnip green.
   Everybody calls it poke salad.
      (Tony Joe White, "Poke Salad Annie")*

Let's face it, Louisianians eat some pretty strange things, things that most people would throw back. But our recipes are usually irresistible to non-Louisianians who make the effort to try them—like fried alligator. Poke salad is...well, how should I say...a culinary dare. Do you consider yourself a world-class gastronome? Do you lie awake wondering exactly what Tony Joe White's straight-razor totin' woman carried home every night and ate for supper? Then the gauntlet has been tossed, and you are *honor-bound* to attend Blanchard's Poke Salad Festival!

Poke salad (also called pokeweed) grows abundantly in moist climates, often reaching a height of 12 feet. It has smooth, long

Poke Salad Parade rider with large poke salad plant on his tailgate

*Tony Joe White, native of Oak Grove, Louisiana, earned fame not only for "Poke Salad Annie," but for writing "Rainy Night in Georgia," which became a hit for Brook Benton in 1970.

leaves and small white flowers. The berries are deep purple and contain seeds that are, like the roots, poisonous. In earlier days, the juice of the berries was used to make ink. The only part of the plant that can be eaten is the young shoots, and those only if boiled long enough to remove the acids.

Poke salad cooked Louisiana style is like a cross between spinach and mustard greens, but coarser. The helping I got at the Poke Salad Festival had bits of meat and an assortment of seasonings, and I must say, I enjoyed it. The platter came with generous portions of cornbread and white beans, so I didn't leave hungry either.

The Caddo Parish village of Blanchard didn't set out to venerate poke salad. Mayor John Rusca intended to have a one-time celebration to recognize the numerous civic improvement projects that came to fruition in 1975. The original title of the festival was "Progress Day." But an astute newspaper editor advised festival organizers to select a catchy name to draw wide-spread attention. Ed Carter, President of the Kiwanis Club, saw a large patch of poke salad on his property one afternoon, and the rest is history.

The festival is held in early May. Parades, rides, food booths (serving poke salad but many other types of food as well), arts and crafts, live music, a horse show, and a street dance are featured. Blanchard is a gracious community that goes out of its way to be hospitable, so you're sure to enjoy yourself. And don't forget, when it comes to the humble plant that gave this festival its name, *you have been dared!* If I tried it, so can you!

Blanchard is about seven miles northwest of Shreveport on La. 173. Take the La. 173 exit from the I-220 bypass loop and follow it straight into town. For further information, call (318) 929-2839.

CELEBRATION OF L'OMELETTE GÉANTE
Abbeville

It's November in Abbeville. Leaves are beginning to fall, the sky is robin's egg blue, and the tantalizing aroma of a 5,000-egg omelet fills the air.

Every year since 1985, the *Confrérie des Chevaliers de l'Omelette Géante d'Abbeville* has convened in Abbeville to prepare the most stupendous omelet in the United States. Astounded onlookers from all over Louisiana and several foreign countries gather to watch the hard-working chevaliers create their masterpiece and—best of all—to taste it!

The scale of this giant omelet is hard to visualize. Imagine trying to follow the recipe:

THE GREAT CAJUN OMELET

5,000 small eggs	52 pounds butter
3½ small sacks medium onions, chopped	6½ gallons milk
75 green bell peppers	4 gallons chopped green onion tops
1½ gallons pure vegetable oil	2 gallons finely chopped fresh parsley
	Tabasco Pepper Sauce (season to taste)

Sauté onions and green peppers in oil until tender, drain excess oil and set aside. In 12-foot skillet, melt butter. Add sautéed vegetables and stir with 8-foot oak paddles. Combine eggs with milk, Tabasco Pepper Sauce and green onion tops. Pour egg mixture into skillet with melted butter. Stir gently as eggs begin to thicken. Top with parsley. For extra flavor, top with sautéed crawfish tails and slivers of marinated beef. Serve with hot French bread.

The *chevaliers* (a group of five to seven people) pre-crack all the eggs for the omelet and carry the prepared ingredients to the cooking site in a triumphant procession. The 12-foot skillet is heated by a wood fire, so timing is of the essence.

The tradition of a festival based on a large omelet was imported to Louisiana by a group of representatives from Abbeville who, on a trip to France, witnessed the Easter Omelet Festival in the small town of Bessières. Long ago, Napoleon Bonaparte persuaded the people of that town to feed his armies with a giant omelet made from eggs gathered around the countryside. Thereafter the townspeople established this tradition as a way to feed the poor.

Chevaliers sauté vegetables and crawfish in butter.

Giant omelet festivals are held not only in Abbeville, but in Dumbea, New Caledonia (an island east of Australia in the South Pacific); Granby, Canada; Frejus, France; and Turin, Italy. Knighted *chevaliers* from each of these cities form part of a brotherhood devoted to international exchange and understanding.

Quibblers might protest that the Abbeville omelet isn't the largest of all time. That may be technically true, but it's by all odds the largest made on an ongoing basis. The 1994 *Guinness Book of Records* documents an omelet made by the Sunrise Jaycees in Las Vegas, Nevada, in October, 1986, with 54,000+ eggs and 531 pounds of cheese. Note the bland recipe and the fact that they only did it *once*.

The Celebration of l'Omelette Géante has something for everyone. Events include an "egg catch" contest, parades, theater, live music, and a tour of local homes on a trolley car. For information on exact dates and times, call the Abbeville Tourist Information Center (318) 898-4264.

FROG FESTIVAL

Rayne

"Ils sont partis!" the announcer says, and off they go. Or maybe they don't. Or maybe they go in the opposite direction. The enthusiastic crowd applauds no matter what happens.

They're not thoroughbreds, they're frogs, the reluctant *raisons d'être* of the annual Rayne Frog Festival. Since 1973, the city of Rayne has held a festival to honor the creature that gave its economy a jump-start (no pun intended) in the early 20th century. The feature attraction, a frog race, is a sight that must be seen to be believed.

Each frog is sponsored by a human who tries to persuade him across the finish line before the rest. "Competitors" must be full-grown bullfrogs measuring at least four inches from head to toe (excluding legs). Tiny green pond frogs are not eligible. Sponsors are permitted to prod their animals once at the starting whistle, but not afterwards. To keep the frogs hopping on course, sponsors may blow on them, pour water or other fluids on them, make loud noises, or strike the concrete with noisy objects. Contestants may not feed their own frogs Tabasco sauce or red pepper to make them jump farther; likewise, they may not sabotage opponents' frogs by feeding them rice, soybeans, or (we assume) quail shot to slow them down.

Local political candidates run the first race. Terrified at the cosmic responsibility thrust onto their shoulders, the frogs often leap for safety into the crowd. Festival attendants catch them and re-spot them on the track. Some competitors freeze under pressure and never budge. Politicians understandably bite their nails over these races. Children of different age groups and adults run heats later.

The races are exciting, but don't forget to stroll around the fairgrounds. Visitors can enjoy

Young political campaigner holds competition frog.

an assortment of foods, rides, crafts, souvenirs, and carnival games. If you're lucky, you can see the Frog Queen at the fairgrounds wearing her crown and gold costume.

Rayne is known as "The Frog Capital of the World," and not without reason. Frogs have always been plentiful in the area. In the 1920s, the Jacques Weil Company of Rayne began exporting frogs for scientific experimentation and dining. Frog exportation became a bedrock industry of the town.

Be sure to take a drive around the city while you're there. Rayne is also known as "The City of Murals." Numerous brick walls in the downtown area have been transformed into giant windows into the Cajun experience. Swamp scenes predominate, as do gigantic fiddle-playing frogs. Many murals were painted by Robert Dafford, a noted artist who has exhibited works throughout the United States and Europe. Dafford and his crew can illustrate a wall in one day. During festival time, houses, storefronts, and offices are gaily festooned with frog kites and windsocks.

Rayne is located about 18 miles west of Lafayette on I-10. The Frog Festival is held in early September. Call (318) 334-2332 for exact dates and times. Festival lovers won't want to miss this one.

Fanciful mural in Rayne

Plantations

MELROSE PLANTATION
Melrose

About 12 miles south of Natchitoches, on the east side of the Cane River, is a plantation that every history lover (and most everyone else, for that matter) should see. All plantations have unique features; Melrose stands out among singularities.

Melrose is possibly the only plantation to have been owned and managed by a freedwoman of color. In 1742, Marie Thérèse Coincoin was born a slave into the household of Louis Juchereau de St. Denis, first commandant of the French post at Natchitoches. After St. Denis and his wife died, Marie Thérèse was sold to another Frenchman, Claude Thomas Pierre Metoyer, whom historians believe to have fathered ten of Marie Thérèse's fourteen children.

Metoyer freed Marie Thérèse in 1780 and her Franco-African children soon afterwards. He also granted her a small parcel of land. This grant was augmented by a grant from the Spanish king, and then by a series of grants to herself and her children throughout the 1790s and early 1800s. Collectively, these lands formed the present Melrose Plantation.

Marie Thérèse supervised the clearing of land, the raising of cattle, and the cultivation of numerous lucrative cash crops. Contemporaries regarded her as intelligent and energetic. In her life of 73 years, she attained a level of self-reliance and prosperity that was not to be open to women or African-Americans until well into the 20th century.

Another strong woman, Cammie Henry, came to Melrose in 1898. She was married to John Hampton Henry, a farmer who is credited with planting Melrose's pecan trees. From the outset she determined to make Melrose a hub of artistic endeavor. She invited writers, artists, and craftspeople of all types to stay at the plantation free of charge, the only stipulation being that they remain productive. Authors such as William Faulkner, John Steinbeck, Sherwood Anderson, Lyle Saxon, Frances Parkinson Keyes, Erskine Caldwell, and Alexander Woollcott all spent time at Melrose.

Miss Cammie also liked to nurture talent wherever she found it. Her greatest discovery was folk artist Clementine Hunter, who came to Melrose at age 15 and worked as a field hand and cook through age 40. One day she found a few discarded paint tubes, squeezed a few extra drops out of them, and "marked a painting." Miss Cammie was intrigued with what she saw and encouraged Clementine to continue.

Clementine Hunter's paintings depicted a vanishing way of life, the arduous but joyous life of a plantation worker she experienced in her youth. Irony, humor, and wisdom suffused her work. She received recognition throughout the art world and did solo shows in New York, Los Angeles, and other cities. The upper floor of the African House at Melrose is a gallery showcasing some of her larger works. Ms. Hunter died on January 1, 1988 at nearly 99 years of age.

Large narrative paintings by Clementine Hunter on display in the African House at Melrose Plantation

To get to Melrose, take I-49 to Cloutierville (exit 119, La. 119). Cross the Cane River and follow La. 119 north to Melrose. Hours are 12:00 noon to 4:00 p.m. daily. Modest admission charged. For further information, call (318) 379-0055 or (318) 379-2431.

THE MYRTLES
St. Francisville

At The Myrtles, you can see 300-pound French chandeliers, mercury-filled glass doorknobs, 19th-century blind-stitch upholstery, and elegant exterior landscaping. But if that's the reason you go, you're missing the whole point.

The point is: Spectral handprints inside a ten-foot mirror; paintings knocked off walls by poltergeists; overnight guests being awakened by the noise of non-existent children playing in the hallway; cats whose images don't appear in photographs.... The point is: *ghosts*.

This stately plantation home in West Feliciana Parish seems to have been built from a blueprint for haunting. Early builders disturbed an ancient Indian burial ground to make way for the original structure in about 1796. Judge Clark Woodruff built The Myrtles as we know it on the same site in 1830. Legend has it that Mr. Woodruff, then age 35, married a girl of 14; they had three children. As was a common practice with wealthy plantation owners, Mr. Woodruff took a slave girl as a mistress. One night this girl was caught eavesdropping on family business. To

The Myrtles by day

teach her a lesson, Mr. Woodruff cut off her right ear. Shocked and humiliated, she immediately began scheming to restore herself to the family's good graces. It so happened that one of the children was having a birthday a few days later. The girl plotted to poison the child's cake—not lethally, just enough to make her painfully sick, so that she could nurse the child back to health and prove her worth to the family.

The poison she chose was oleander. Oleander is a highly deadly poison that is difficult to detect even with modern chemical analysis. The slave girl unfortunately put in too much, and two of the children died. An angry mob murdered the slave girl shortly thereafter.

The custom in the early 1800s was to wake bodies in the parlor. Superstition held that mirrors had to be covered with black velvet to prevent disembodied spirits from becoming trapped in them. During the wakes following these three deaths, all mirrors at The Myrtles were duly covered—except the large mirror in the foyer. In this mirror you can see black smudges which are believed to be the handprints of the slave girl and the two murdered children. Although the glass has been cleaned and replaced several times, *the handprints always reappear.*

A subsequent owner of the plantation was shot by an unknown gunman. He tried to climb the stairs to reach his wife, but collapsed on the 17th step. Visitors often report losing their footing on that step.

In 1927, a caretaker was murdered on the plantation. His very solid apparition occasionally greets guests at the gate.

The Myrtles' reputation for unearthly visitations recently earned it the title of "Thirteenth Most Haunted House in America," a ranking the staff relishes. During the filming of the 1985 TV movie, *The Long Hot Summer*, the cast and crew became so unnerved by unexplained occurrences that they moved about the house and grounds in groups for protection.

Many more eerie tales await you at The Myrtles. Take the "Mystery Tour" at 8:30 on Friday or Saturday night if you're a fan of late-night ghost stories. The tour takes one hour. Admission charged. Crowds can be large, so plan to arrive early. Overnight stays are available for those brave enough to sleep there (the rooms are really quite charming).

The Myrtles is located on U.S. 61 just north of St. Francisville. For more information, call (504) 635-6277.

Museums

EMY-LOU BIEDENHARN FOUNDATION

Monroe

Monroe is home to one of Louisiana's most unusual museums: the Emy-Lou Biedenharn Bible Museum. Behind its 700-pound bronze front door (precision balanced to open effortlessly) is an exhibit of Bibles and rare books that will fascinate bibliophiles as well as casual observers.

Emy-Lou Biedenharn began collecting Bibles when her father, Joseph Biedenharn, presented her with an original Wycliffe New Testament in 1939. She later acquired a 1611 King James Bible, a 1560 Geneva Bible, a 1568 Bishops' Bible, and a 1763 new-world translation of the Bible into Algonquin. All are on permanent display.

The "Gun Wad Bible" has a curious legend. Its leaves were printed in Germantown, Pennsylvania, in 1763, but never bound. Soldiers strapped for supplies allegedly tore them into strips and used them for gun wadding. The museum holds some of the intact leaves.

Of interest to book lovers is the 1640 *Bay Psalm Book*, the first book printed in what would become the United States. Don't overlook the 1876 Julia Smith Bible, the first translation known to be made by a woman. Julia Smith, fiercely independent and accomplished in several classical languages, was decades ahead of her time.

There's a lot more than books at the Biedenharn Foundation. Joseph Biedenharn, Emy-Lou's father, developed the bottling process for Coca-Cola in 1894. His study has a display of early Coca-Cola bottles and promotional products. Emy-Lou was a contralto who performed in Europe prior to World War II; on the tour, you'll see memorabilia from her illustrious career. She also had a passion for art objects and fine furnishings, neither of which is in short supply in the Biedenharn home. ELsong Garden and Conservatory are extravagantly landscaped and cry out to be photographed.

Tours are free and begin on the hour, 10:00 a.m. to 4:00 p.m. Tuesday through Friday, 2:00 p.m. to 4:00 p.m. Saturday and Sunday. Appointments required for groups of ten or more. The address is 2006 Riverside Drive, Monroe. Call 1-800-362-0983 or (318) 387-5281 for further information.

Emy-Lou Biedenharn Foundation

MUSEUM OF HISTORIC NATCHITOCHES

Natchitoches

Eighty thousand years before man first set foot in North America, when the Pleistocene ice age was still in full swing, when the technology of making tools out of chipped stones was considered cutting-edge—this *thing* came into being. This *thing* is 30 x 27 x 16 inches and weighs 113 pounds, and it looks something like a meteorite. This *thing* at the front of the Museum of Historical Natchitoches is a 100,000 year-old pine knot.

"Knothead," as it is affectionately known, was found in a swamp 50 miles east of Natchitoches in 1914. Scientists believe it was able to resist petrification and decomposition because of its high resin content. Its numerous whorls and striations give it an eerie, otherworldly appearance. Daniel Graves, owner and curator of the Museum of Historical Natchitoches, is justly proud of this piece.

Daniel Graves with "Knothead"

But visually arresting as it is, "Knothead" is not the only reason to visit the museum. The building itself is believed to have been part of the underground railroad in pre-Civil War days. (Look for the mysterious downward-leading stairway with no door at the bottom.) Mr. Graves has also assembled an impressive Civil War display focusing on the Red River Campaign of 1864.

Many big studio movies have been filmed in Natchitoches. John Wayne, John Ford, and William Holden came to town in 1959 to shoot *The Horse Soldiers.* Shirley Maclaine, Olympia Dukakis, Sally Field, Dolly Parton, and Darryl Hannah came in 1988 for *Steel Magnolias.* Sam Waterston starred in a splendid but little-known 1991 film set in Natchitoches, *The Man in the Moon.* Mr. Graves has memorabilia from all these movies on permanent display, including a bridesmaid's dress from *Steel Magnolias.*

The museum is loaded with artifacts from northwest Louisiana's past. One example is a doctor's bag, complete with implements and medicines, from the late 1800s. Another is a set of infant footprints in fired clay with the inscription "9/1/1756"; the block of clay was being used as a bookend in a private home. Both are now on display in the museum. He also rescued an ornate wrought-iron handrail from a trash heap last year. He later learned that it was from Willow Plantation, circa 1812. Ask Mr. Graves to show you his collection of original newspapers from the 19th and early 20th centuries.

Natchitoches has myriad attractions. To get a good overview of the city and the Cane River area, watch Mr. Graves's 20-minute video. He wrote, directed, and filmed the video himself, and can answer most any question you might have about the area. The museum makes a great first stop.

To get there, take I-49 to exit 119 (La. 6). Ride La. 6 through the brick-paved downtown area (a great drive), and look for the museum on the left just after the pavement changes back to cement. Admission charged. For more information, call (318) 357-0070.

CIVIL WAR NAVAL MUSEUM

Arcadia

Bill Atteridge is quick to point out that the *Monitor* and the *Merrimack*, the Civil War's two best-known battleships, had comparatively dull careers. "They fought to a draw," he says. "Every other ship in this museum is more interesting."

He constructed faithful models of the *Monitor* and *Merrimack* anyway, as well as dozens of other Civil War battleships. The Civil War Naval Museum in Arcadia houses the largest, and arguably finest, collection of Civil War ship models in the world. These models aren't plastic and don't come from boxes. They come from Bill Atteridge's painstaking historical research and precision craftsmanship.

Years ago, while working as a sales manager for a mobile home factory, Mr. Atteridge visited a Civil War museum in Vicksburg and was captivated by a replica of the *Cairo* he saw there. He asked if he could buy a model kit of it, but was told none existed. Major toy manufacturers were not interested in developing a kit, so Mr. Atteridge created a model of his own.

The rest is, so to speak, history. Civil War battleships began consuming more of his time and living space, so he built a museum at the front of his property and retired from the mobile home business. True to form, he built a scale model of the museum first, and referred to it constantly to make sure everything was coming out right. The task took him two-and-a-half years working one day a week. Now he is full-time curator of the museum.

Listen closely to Mr. Atteridge's account of the evolution of the Civil War Navy. It sounds like a suspense novel. At the outset of the war, there was no navy to speak of. Paddlewheelers, barges, and civilian craft of all types were modified and drafted into military service. Vessels had to be towed to river docks and retooled by local craftsmen—whoever happened to be on hand at the time. Outfitting expertise varied widely, and precise plans were rarely drawn.

The earliest warships of the period were *timber clads*, meaning that their hulls were made of wood. Timber clads were so vulnerable to cannon fire that a variety of experimental reinforcement configurations were introduced, including *tin clad*, *rubber clad*,

Bill Atteridge

and finally *iron clad*. The *Monitor* and *Merrimack* were iron clads.

Photography was in its infancy in the 1860s. Matthew Brady and other early photojournalists focused on land campaigns, so there is little precise information to be found about individual ships. Thus, Mr. Atteridge must carefully evaluate descriptions of each ship from soldiers' diaries, letters, newspaper articles, and contemporary engravings before designing a model.

Every ship tells a story. For example, the world's first combat submarine, a crude prototype of which was first used in the Civil War, went to the bottom three times before being scrapped. Another battleship fired such a ferocious cannonade at Confederates troops that they couldn't cross the James River at the Battle of Shiloh. The C.S.S. *Calhoun*, a privateer vessel, was so efficient that it was pressed into the service of both the Confederacy and the Union at various times during the war. Ram ships, which carried only light firepower, sank more vessels by staving (smashing holes into) them than conventional battleships did by shooting them.

Mr. Atteridge believes firmly that the navy played a crucial role in the Civil War, though its importance is often overlooked. Civil War buffs and casual observers alike will enjoy hearing his informative presentation.

Take I-20 to exit 69 (Arcadia). Go north to Parish Road 195. Turn left. Go to the first stop sign, then turn right and follow the road around to the blue and white museum building. Admission is free, but donations are accepted. Hours are 10:00 a.m. to 4:30 p.m. Thursday through Saturday, and 1:00 p.m. to 4:30 p.m. on Sunday.

LOUISIANA POLITICAL MUSEUM AND HALL OF FAME
Winnfield

At the Louisiana Political Museum in Winnfield, a huge diorama is devoted to former governor Huey P. Long. By *huge*, I mean two or three times as large as any other inductee's—just how Huey would have liked it. Larger than life, but larger in death than he was in life, Huey Long once drew national attention to Louisiana with his revolutionary fiscal programs and his shocking assassination.

What better site for a museum about Louisiana politics than Winnfield, birthplace of the Long dynasty and cradle of the "peapatch politics" movement? Aware of its place in history, the city of Winnfield converted an old railroad depot into a gallery of political heroes, starting with the Kingfish himself and working its way forward to the present. You can be sure there's no shortage of personalities.

There's Earl K. Long, brother and early rival of Huey, who did a great deal to improve race relations in Louisiana despite an infamous liaison with Blaze Starr and numerous bouts with insanity. When confined at East Louisiana State Hospital in Mandeville, "Uncle Earl" fired the superintendent of the hospital and replaced him with someone who would sign his release papers.

An old train depot now houses Winnfield's Political Museum.

There's "Coozan" Dudley LeBlanc, representative from Vermilion Parish and early proponent of the social security program, who is best known for inventing the patent medicine Hadacol and promoting it in whistlestop tours across the South.

There's Jimmie Davis, the "Singing Governor," who campaigned by singing country songs and had a worldwide hit in the 1940s with "You Are My Sunshine." And there's B. B. "Sixty" Rayburn of Bogalusa, who has served in the state house of representatives continuously since 1948. There's Victor Bussie, head of the AFL-CIO, not an elected official but often considered the most powerful man in the state.

And of course there's four-term Governor Edwin Edwards—flashy, glib, incendiary, but tremendously effective with the legislature. History will record him as the most popular Louisiana governor of all time despite his nearly constant involvement in controversy.

There are many more fascinating exhibits. Exhibits include rare photographs, newspaper clippings, campaign buttons, bumper stickers, leaflets, and caricatures. Caricatures were drawn by Louisiana cartoonist Preston A. "Pap" Dean, whose early frames appeared in the LSU *Daily Reveille* in the 1930s and whose lifetime achievement earned him a place in the museum.

The museum was built over a five-year period with volunteer and vo-tech labor from the Winnfield area. Doors first opened in April, 1993. Items on display were donated by non-profit groups. A special ceremony is held whenever a new figure is inducted. The museum will continue to expand as long as Louisiana continues to produce noteworthy politicians. An adjoining museum features World War II exhibits, including uniforms, newspapers, flags, medals, and photographs taken in Louisiana during the war years.

"After you get a Ph.D. in political science, you should go to Louisiana for a post-graduate course," an astute out-of-state observer said. Visit the Louisiana political museum for a peek at the syllabus.

Admission is free. Take La. 167 north from Alexandria to Winnfield. The museum is 2 blocks off 167; ask any of the friendly natives for directions, or call (318) 628-5928 for further information. Hours are 10:00 a.m. to 4:00 p.m., Tuesday through Saturday.

TOUCHSTONE WILDLIFE & ART MUSEUM

Bossier City

TOP TEN REASONS TO VISIT SAM TOUCHSTONE'S
MUSEUM INSTEAD OF A REGULAR ZOO

10) No insect bites
 9) No overpriced concessions
 8) Exhibits never close for remodeling
 7) Kids never tempted to tease animals
 6) No pesky animal rights protesters
 5) Pricey train ride not an option
 4) Gas mask not needed when you pass by the reptile exhibit
 3) Air-cooled comfort
 2) Admission cheaper by several dollars
 1) Animals don't hibernate after meals

"Stuffed" is a four-letter word at Sam Touchstone's Wildlife
and Art Museum. Mr. Touchstone was around in the days when
taxidermy was hardly more than a hobby, a macabre technique of

Entrance to "zooseum"

preserving family pets and mounting felled hunting quarry. He's done a lot to bring taxidermy out of the dark ages, and his "zoo-seum" on La. 80 in Bossier City is a monument to his accomplishment.

For a mere $1.00, you can see a 300-pound gorilla, a Siberian tiger, an African lion, an Alaskan polar bear, numerous owls, fowl, rodents, reptiles, zebras—over 1,000 animals in all. A special diorama contains waterfowl, frogs, turtles, nutria, and other inhabitants of Louisiana's marshlands.

All animals are sited in true-to-life backgrounds donated by local artists. Working as a team, Mr. Touchstone and his artists strive to depict creatures in their natural habitats doing characteristic things. Some creatures are not behind glass. These can—and *should!*—be petted: "Please Touch!" say the signs. Though there's no elephant, there is an elephant *skull*, which of course can be touched.

The museum showcases more than just animals. Fascinating collections of World War II ammunition, arrowheads, and insects from the South Pacific round out the tour. Be sure to see the cast of the shrunken human head. Like any zoo, but unlike most museums, cameras are welcome.

Mr. Touchstone got started in taxidermy over half a century ago. He developed a number of taxidermy products superior to those already on the market, and started a flourishing mail-order business. In 1983, he was inducted into the National Hall of Fame of the National Taxidermist Association. Mr. Touchstone obtains most of his animal skins from zoos after animals die, though he occasionally goes on a safari. He takes pride in the fact that his museum is privately funded and did not cost one tax dollar to build.

If you're tired of the bustle and inconvenience of zoos but enjoy observing wildlife, make it a point to visit this *touchstone* of museum excellence. The museum is located on the south side of La. 80, about 2 miles east of Louisiana Downs in Bossier City. For more information, call (318) 949-2323.

"Please Touch!" say the signs.

W. H. TUPPER GENERAL MERCHANDISE MUSEUM/ TELEPHONE PIONEER MUSEUM

Jennings

At the W. H. Tupper General Merchandise Museum, you won't see dioramas, artists' reconstructions, timelines, or placards. You won't need them. The articles you see on shelves and in glass cases represent the full, intact inventory of a general store that shut its doors over 50 years ago.

W. H. Tupper opened for business in 1910. Farmers were his original clientele; but as the economy began to prosper, the demand for increasingly diverse consumer goods grew, and so did Mr. Tupper's customer base. Sales continued brisk through the '30s and '40s, until advances in transportation enabled rural residents to seek out glamorous shops in distant metropolitan areas.

The store closed for good in 1949. The stock remained on the shelves undisturbed until 1971, when Celia, one of Tupper's

1949 groceries with 1949 prices

daughters, boxed it up and moved it to an adjoining warehouse. Joe Tupper, Jr., Tupper's grandson, donated the contents of the warehouse to the City of Jennings in 1989. The city consulted with experts who helped them restock the shelves as they most likely were in 1949.

All articles on display were manufactured in or before 1949. Many are in their original, unopened packaging. You can see corsets, hats, chewing gum, dolls, toys, medicines and tonics, garden tools, cooking utensils, canned goods, and much more. Visiting this museum is like stepping into a three-dimensional black-and-white photograph.

But there's more to see. At the rear of the W. H. Tupper Museum is another attraction, the Louisiana Telephone Pioneers Museum. The Telephone Pioneers is a society of telephone employees founded in 1911 to promote excellence in telephone service. The goals were later broadened to include volunteer work. A short film introduces you to the Pioneers and gives a fascinating account of the evolution of telecommunications, especially as it relates to Louisiana. Another film gives a brief history of the Cajuns.

Displays consist of antique telephones, telegraphs, teletype machines, phone booths, telephone tools, and wartime communications gear. There's also a re-creation of Alexander Graham Bell's laboratory.

A modest admission is charged at the beginning, but you get two museums for the price of one. Plus, you may be greeted at the door by the fattest cat in Southwest Louisiana.

To get to the W. H. Tupper General Merchandise Museum, take I-10 to Jennings (midway between Lafayette and Lake Charles). Exit at La. 26 (exit 64) and head south. Turn left at U.S. 90 and follow it to Main Street. Go through several intersections to Plaquemine Street. The museum is at 311 North Main Street, near the corner of Main and Plaquemine. Call (318) 821-5532 for more information.

Micro-Chapels

ST. MICHAEL'S CHURCH
LOURDES GROTTO
Convent

Unless you know about it beforehand, you probably won't notice what's at the rear of St. Michael the Archangel Church in Convent. No signs advertise it, and the building's imposing Gothic/ Roman façade hardly lets on that there's a stunning work of religious folk art inside.

In 1876, St. Michael's parishioners Florian Dicharry and Christophe Colombe built a scale replica of the grotto in southern France where the Blessed Virgin Mary appeared to Bernadette Soubirous in 1858. What makes the Louisiana grotto unique, aside from its splendid craftsmanship, is that it was made almost entirely with *bagasse*.

Bagasse is a brick-like substance yielded when sugarcane is refined into sugar. Through the late 19th century, it was widely used as a building material in the marshlands and swamps of South Louisiana. Rap your knuckles on one of the *clinkers* (bagasse bricks) at the Lourdes Grotto and you'll see why local builders relied on it.

Resourceful Dicharry and Colombe cemented the clinkers together around an inverted sugar kettle. In a recessed area of their bagasse cliff, they placed a small wooden altar covered with hundreds of tiny clamshells, each of which they attached with a single nail. A statue of Mary looks down on the altar. Behind the bagasse structure is a scene painted to resemble the countryside around Lourdes.

The choice of bagasse was no mere coincidence. Dicharry and Colombe's sturdy concretion of clinkers closely resembles the rocky backdrop of the real site near the Pyrenees in southern

France. All told, the grotto in St. Michael's is an amazingly faithful copy. St. Michael's is believed to be the first church in the U.S. to install such a shrine.

St. Michael the Archangel Church was built from 1831 to 1833 with slave labor. A pipe organ was added in 1857. The majestic altar was imported from France in 1868. Though added later, the Lourdes Grotto behind the altar seems to evoke an earlier time, when miracles were more immediate and religion was closer to the surface of everyday life. The scores of devotional candles and thank-you letters to the Blessed Mother suggest that strong religious faith still has a place in our day and time.

St. Michael the Archangel Church is on River Road (La. 44) in eastern St. James Parish. Take I-10 to La. 70 (the Sunshine Bridge exit) and follow the signs to the River Road. The church is about 10 miles south on the left.

Lourdes Grotto at St. Michael the Archangel Church

SMITH'S MEMORIAL SHRINE

Near Golden Meadow

It's only 8-feet high, 10-feet wide, and 14-feet deep, but it's got a lot of heart. Frequent visitors to Grand Isle are well acquainted with this distinctive landmark 2½ miles south of Golden Meadow on La. 1. Noonie Smith erected the shrine in 1971 to commemorate the untimely deaths of her two sons.

Livingston Smith died of encephalitis at age three in 1947. Abraham J. Smith, Jr., died of stab wounds at age 16 in 1966. Though suspects were apprehended, no convictions were ever made in the case. A grief-stricken Ms. Smith decided to apply her energies to a constructive project, and Smith's Memorial Shrine was the result.

A plain white clapboard exterior disguises a densely furnished interior. There are four pews, each wide enough to hold two people. The altar has a crucifix, a Latin Bible, statues of the Blessed Virgin Mary, and photographs of Ms. Smith's sons. Over the years, generous visitors have donated many articles, including the kneeler in front of the altar and numerous religious statues. All

Smith's Memorial Shrine

fourteen stations of the cross are represented, and devotional candles crowd the altar.

Noonie Smith currently operates a gift shop, Noonie's Imports, on the west side of La. 1 opposite the shrine. The shrine was originally on the west side of the street also, but she moved it across the street so she wouldn't forget to close the door whenever it rained; the door to the chapel is never locked. Ms. Smith intends it as a place of refuge for travelers. Sunday morning fishermen might consider dropping by if they can't make it to church later in the day.

A couple recently celebrated their 60th wedding anniversary by renewing their vows in the shrine. Because of its uniqueness as a religious structure, it has been featured in *Ripley's Believe It or Not!* as well as many newspapers.

Whether you're religious or not, you'll find this shrine a fascinating addition to any trip to Grand Isle.

Smith's Memorial Shrine is about 55 miles south of Thibodaux on La. 1.

MADONNA CHAPEL

Point Pleasant

SMALLEST CHURCH
IN THE WORLD
MADONNA CHAPEL

Technically, the Madonna Chapel isn't the smallest church in the world.   The 1994 *Guinness Book of Records* lists two smaller: the Chapel of Santa Isabel de Hungría in Benálmadena, Málaga, Spain, which has irregular sides and a floor area of 21.125 square feet; and the Cross Island Chapel in Oneida, New York, with sides 6'9½" and 4'3½" and a floor area of 29.1 square feet.   The Madonna Chapel, measuring 8' by 8' and covering 64 square feet, seems like a cathedral by comparison.

Madonna Chapel, Point Pleasant

Yet, it's hard to imagine what meaningful religious observances those two smaller churches could support. Cross Island Chapel, the larger of the two, has only slightly more floor area than a twin-sized bed. That doesn't leave much room for an altar, a prayer book, or even a priest. The Madonna Chapel, on the other hand, has an altar, a holy water stand, and room for four or perhaps five people to pray. (More would be awkward.) Each year on August 15, a mass is held there in honor of the Assumption of the Blessed Virgin Mary. Not surprisingly, the crowd soon spills over into the lawn. Because of its functionality, the Madonna Chapel transcends the merely ornamental.

The chapel was erected in about 1903 by a poor Italian sugar farmer named Anthony Gullo. When his son fell seriously ill, he vowed to build a chapel to the Madonna if the boy could be restored to health. The boy recovered, and the chapel was built. It was renovated in 1924 and has remained essentially unchanged since. Travelers from France, Germany, England, Belgium, Mexico, Guatemala, and all fifty states have paid visits to this photogenic chapel.

Madonna Chapel is surrounded by a chain link fence, but the gate is always open. If you find the front door to the chapel locked, check in the wooden mailbox to the right of the door for a key.

The chapel is located on La. 405 (River Road) in the community of Point Pleasant, a few miles north of the rear entrance to Nottoway Plantation. Take La. 1 to Plaquemine and turn left at La. 75. Go through one stoplight then turn right on La. 405. The Chapel of the Madonna is about 10 miles down on the right.

ROCK CHAPEL
Carmel

Secluded is the best word to describe the Rock Chapel. It's at the end of a winding clay-and-gravel road, behind a locked gate, and across a wooden foot bridge. Beyond it is forest.

That's exactly how the Carmelite monks who erected the chapel in 1891 would have wanted it. They built the exterior with large rocks gathered from the area. Monks from France painted the exquisite murals and frescoes on the interior. Present-day visitors can rest assured that no one will find them there but their traveling companions and God.

The Rock Chapel is all that survives of a once-thriving Carmelite monastery. The Very Reverend Anastasius Peters arrived in the tiny DeSoto Parish village of Bayou Pierre in 1886. He established a church settlement there which, at its peak, included a two-story wooden monastery, a bakery, a post office, and even a convent for Carmelite sisters. Bayou Pierre changed its name to Carmel in 1889 in honor of the accomplishments of the monks.

Sickness and poverty de-cimated the ministry in the 1890s. Survivors were forced to assume the respon-sibilities of several people; morale plummeted. A fire gutted the main monastery building in 1895. Shortly thereafter, the Carmelite sisters left, and the church settlement was vacated. A giant fire in 1904 spared only the Rock Chapel and one other building.

From 1904 to 1959, the Rock Chapel languished in isolation. Father William Kwaaitaal, another Carmelite,

A wooden bridge leads to the Rock Chapel.

undertook to have it renovated in 1959. It was rededicated in 1961 and has seen steady streams of visitors since then.

The grounds around the chapel are clean and inviting. The interior paintings are exquisite, but you must open the front door wide to see them clearly, as the windows are tiny and there's no electric lighting. Silence and serenity prevail here.

The Rock Chapel is unique in having been built entirely of native stone. Its endurance despite the ravages of fire and prolonged neglect make it a symbol of persistence in the face of adversity. Those seeking a few moments of meditation should pay the Rock Chapel a visit.

You must first pick up a set of keys at Laffitte Store. One key opens the gate, the other key opens the heavy front doors. Ask the clerk at the store for precise directions to the chapel. The easiest way to get to Carmel is to take I-49 to La. 509 (exit 172) and go west. Turn left at the first major road (look for a sign that says "Carmel Gourmet Hamburgers"). Follow that road to Laffitte Store.

Interior of Rock Chapel

Collectors

JIMMY "PATCHES"
Minden

When Boy Scout patches began to overrun his Minden home, Jimmy Rogers did the only sensible thing: he built a museum in his back yard.

There, curious travelers can see over 2,500 Boy Scout patches spanning four continents and six decades. Mr. Rogers (known as Jimmy "Patches" to collectors) boasts one of the largest collections of Boy Scout patches and memorabilia in the United States, larger even than the National Museum of Scouting in Kentucky.

Mr. Rogers has been involved in scouting for 57 years. A local pastor invited him to be a scoutmaster, and he's served in a volunteer capacity ever since. He began collecting patches in 1961. His oldest piece is a 1940 patch from nearby Camp Caddo. Among his more striking holdings are patches from Camp Yatasi, Caney Lake, Puerto Rico, and Japan. He has souvenir patches from virtually every American Jamboree and many international ones. Glass cases covering the walls are filled with merit badges (American and Canadian), sashes, neck slides, neckerchiefs, pins, and buttons. A head-to-toe 1949 uniform is on display. Another attention-grabber is a "Scouting in Space" patch which was carried aboard the Apollo-Soyuz Mission in 1975.

But scouting memorabilia isn't the only thing to see. Mr. Rogers also collects law enforcement patches, ancient arrowheads, foreign currency (especially occupation currency), and autographs. A World War II veteran who stays active in church and Civitan, he's rubbed shoulders with the likes of Suzy Boguss, Marie Osmond, and former world heavyweight champion Archie

Jimmy Rogers with just a few of his Boy Scout patches

Moore. Photographs of Mr. Rogers with these celebrities are sandwiched into the already crowded glass cases.

During the 1950s, Mr. Rogers played center field for Minden's semi-pro team, the Redbirds. His uniform from 1951—the year the Redbirds won the Big 8 championship—is on permanent display, along with numerous major league team-autographed baseballs.

Mr. Rogers estimates the total value of his museum at $15,000. But it's worth far more to anyone who loves scouting, as Mr. Rogers evidently does. Not one square inch of his 19' x 19' museum is wasted. Furthermore, it's no static collection. Mr. Rogers' motto is, "Have Patches, Will Trade." If you own a valuable patch and would like to swap for it, give Mr. Rogers a call. He's also very informative about historical sites in the northwest part of the state, so ask for a few travel tips, too.

Admission is free. Call in advance at (318) 377-0633; Mr. Rogers will give directions. Minden is about 20 miles east of Shreveport on I-20.

CURTIS & NORMA VIZIER'S BOTTLE COLLECTION

Grand Isle

Every bottle has a message in it for Curtis Vizier, and that message is history. He's been gathering antique bottles from the marshes of Grand Isle since 1978, and his home now contains more than 3,000 glass narratives of coastal Louisiana history from the mid-nineteenth century to the present. And that's after giving away 800 to his daughter!

Mr. Vizier (pronounced VEE-ZHAY) found his first bottle on a fishing expedition with a preacher. Curtis didn't think much of it at the time, and gave the bottle to the preacher, who was himself a bottle fancier. Most of those early finds went as gifts to friends. But before long he developed an antiquarian's interest and began collecting in earnest.

The oldest item in his collection is a colorless, flat vial with the words "N. Wood & Son 1843" on the side. From the same era is an 1846 Ponds Extract bottle. Both feel very heavy for their size; consumers nowadays are accustomed to lightweight plastic. Curtis has numerous Civil War beer bottles, each of them hand-made and unique.

The most valuable item in his collection is an olive green Hofstedter bottle which has been appraised at $94. Other showpieces include: a blue 1906 Milk of Magnesia bottle; a full and unopened bottle of the Louisiana-made patent medicine Hadacol; several Coca-Cola bottles from the 1910s; and numerous oyster-encrusted vessels. On the wall in the kitchen is a rack for his collection of "ship bottles," so called because they have rounded bottoms and had to be stored horizontally to keep the corks moist on long voyages.

A small fraction of Curtis Vizier's bottle collection

On September 30, 1893, a deadly hurricane slammed into Grand Isle. Between 900 and 2,000 people perished. No structure on the island was left standing, not even the glamorous Krantz Hotel, where socialites and glitterati of the Gay '90s came to vacation. Curtis and his wife, Norma, have unearthed a complete Krantz Hotel place setting, along with scores of wine bottles and liquor glasses. These pieces remind one of man's vulnerability to the wrath of nature.

Mr. Vizier is an oysterman by trade, but searches for bottles every day. He takes a long, thin pole and pushes it downward into the sand until he hits something. By the vibration in the pole, he can tell if the object is a bottle, a shell, a bone, or something else. He takes great pains not to break potential bottles in the process. In fact, since he started collecting, he's only broken one bottle. "And I almost cried," he said.

The Viziers don't restrict themselves to bottles. They have inkwells, lanterns, marbles, buttons—countless antique items retrieved from the sea—and they enjoy telling the stories behind each piece. Be sure to include them in your next visit to Grand Isle. Call ahead at (504) 787-3475 to make an appointment. They live on Santiny Lane, 16th house from the main highway on the right (no street numbers).

R&K'S OYSTER PLACE

Grand Isle

One morning oysterman Raleigh Lasseigne was pulling a flatboat through the marsh near Grand Isle. He spotted what he thought was the top of a human skull embedded in a reef. With mixed dread and fascination, he began scooping away the sand with his fingers. The deeper he dug, the more relieved he became: it wasn't a skull at all, but a large earthenware urn.

The urn was unlike any he had seen before—primitive in design, asymmetrical. He asked a professor from Nicholls State University in Thibodaux to take a look at it. Imagine Raleigh's astonishment when the professor told him that the urn was at least 200 years old, possibly even 400!

Now the urn hangs from the ceiling in R&K's Oyster Place, Raleigh's seafood store in Grand Isle. No one is certain where it came from or who made it. Knowledgeable customers speculate that it was used to store olive oil, its rounded bottom permitting it to be stacked in hay.

R&K's Oyster Place is full of marshland marvels. Over the

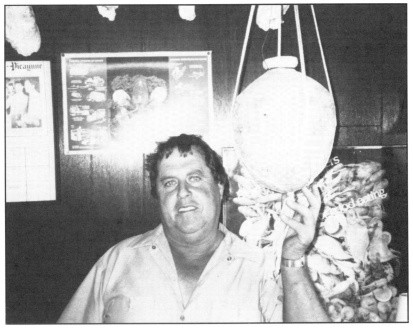

Raleigh Lasseigne with centuries-old urn found in gulf marshes

years Raleigh has found oysters eight, nine, even ten inches long. He calls these "po-boy oysters," because one of them by itself can fill a po-boy bun. He's found numerous oyster clusters, where live oysters naturally fuse themselves into cemented aggregations of 30 or more. On the walls are photographs of Grand Isle taken in 1939.

Both Raleigh and his wife, Kay, are happy to tell stories about the early days of Grand Isle and the many curiosities in their store. Drop in, pick up a bag of fresh oysters, and take a good look around. You won't be disappointed.

R&K's Oyster Place is located on Oak Lane, just off the main highway in Grand Isle. Road signs show the way, but in case you get lost, you can call (504) 787-2444.

Fermenting & Brewing

THE FELICIANA WINE COUNTRY

Napa. Sonoma. Feliciana.

If one of these names doesn't seem to fit, you obviously haven't cruised the Muscadine Miracle Mile on La. 10 near the Mississippi border. Since the early 1990s, two small but amazing wineries have opened in the Feliciana towns of Clinton and Jackson, and they appear destined to put Louisiana on America's wine list.

CASA DE SUE
Clinton

The first to open was Casa De Sue in Clinton. Manly ("Mac") Cazedessus was running a pick-your-own blueberry and muscadine farm that was doing well—too well. An overabundance of blueberries one season led him to experiment with blueberry wine. His "experiment" was so enthusiastically received that he decided to try his hand at muscadine wine.

The rest is history. He went from making 200 gallons with a bucket-sized press the first year (1992) to making 4,000 gallons with imported Italian equipment tin 1994, and he hopes eventually to make 20,000 gallons a year. Casa De Sue's wine list now has seven muscadine and two blueberry varieties, all of which can be sampled for free in the tasting room.

Casa De Sue is entirely owned and operated by family members, and that's how Mac Cazedessus wants it to stay. All blueberries and muscadines are grown organically, and the pulp is

Vineyards at Casa De Sue

used as fertilizer. Each morning Mac opens his 55-gallon drums of fermenting blueberries and presses them down with his bare hands—a "hands-on" technique which releases CO_2 and accelerates the fermenting process. To make his job safer, the innovative Mac has created a polypropylene screen to prevent seeds from shooting out between the slats of small wooden presses.

Mac points out that the muscadine is a hardy native variety of grape which is resistant to many diseases that plague the conventional grape. It also tolerates much more heat and dampness than the conventional grape, which makes it ideal for Louisiana's steamy climate.

At Casa De Sue, you'll get a video introduction, a tour of the facilities, and—the highlight—a free tasting. You won't be disappointed. To get there, take I-55 to exit 53 (La. 10) and drive west for 25 miles. Turn left at Slaton's General Store (Gilead Road). Keep left when the road forks. After the fork, the road is unimproved, so drive carefully. Call 1(800) 683-5937 for more information.

FELICIANA CELLARS

Jackson

The second winery to open was Feliciana Cellars. Visitors to this winery won't have to look for ways to be impressed: the elegant Spanish-style architecture; winemaker James L. Hendrickson's scientific passion for perfection; and of course, the wine.

Founders M. Leroy Harvey, Jr. and Rupert G. Thompson were instrumental in amending Prohibition-era laws that discouraged large-scale winemaking in Louisiana. Their goal was to create an indigenous wine that could complement the best of Louisiana's fine cuisine.

Before they ever planted the first vine, they solicited advice on vineyard and winery management from experts across the country. James L. Hendrickson, a retired U.S. Air Force colonel who joined the team in 1993, gained an appreciation for fine winemaking in Germany, Spain, and the Middle East, as well as throughout the United States. The "mountains of Louisiana" in Clinton were deemed by all to be an ideal site for a winery.

Feliciana Cellars produces three wines: Evangeline, a sweet white made from the Carlos white muscadine; Galvez, a semi-sweet white made from the Carlos bronze muscadine; and Gabriel, a semi-sweet red made from the dark purple/red Noble

Feliciana Cellars

muscadine. White muscadine grapes are cold-aged before being pressed, which intensifies their natural sugar content and reduces the need for yeast. A sweeter wine results. Mr. Hendrickson personally cleans the 1500-gallon stainless steel tanks where the juice is fermented. All wine is filtered twice and stored in sterilized bottles. Mr. Hendrickson runs tests at numerous stages of the fermentation process to monitor clarity, pH, SO_2, and alcohol content. The winery eventually hopes to produce 20,000 barrels per year.

An intriguing feature of Feliciana Cellars is the "cold room," a quonset hut-shaped enclosure under five feet of earth where small drums of peach, blueberry, and strawberry are fermented. Inside you can view the entire winemaking process in miniature. But be warned: it's *cold* in there!

After all the scientific explanations, the tasting finally makes everything come together. If you've never tried muscadine wine before, you're in for a pleasant surprise. Take I-55 to exit 53 (La. 10) and drive about 35 miles west into Jackson; or take I-110 north from Baton Rouge to La. 19, La. 19 north to La. 10, then left on La. 10 about 5 miles. Call (504) 634-7397 or 634-7951 for more information.

The "Cold Room" at Feliciana Cellars

RIKENJAK'S BREWERY

Jackson

At the moment, Rikenjak's beer is hard to find. But that's not the fault of brewmaster Rick Nyberg, who works from 4:30 a.m. till far past sundown just trying to keep up with the orders. An excited group of restaurants and retail outlets in South Louisiana carry the new brew, but they sell out practically as soon as they unload the trucks.

What is it about Rikenjak's that places it in such demand? In recent years, an interest has awakened in fine beer, in quality lager and ale that hasn't been brewed in 100,000-gallon vats for rapid consumption after sweaty work. Reflective beer drinkers are growing in number—connoisseurs who savor every scent and swallow of what they buy. This group has discovered Rikenjak's. You might say it's a thinking man's beer.

Rick Nyberg and Jack Little (RIK and JAK), who formed a partnership in August, 1993, are certainly thinking men's brewers. Both were engineers at Riverbend Nuclear Power Plant who applied their considerable technical skills to the task of brewing. For months, they got together and made home brew in their garages. They were so enthusiastic about the results that they decided to go into business. They converted a building that originally housed a boat trailer into a microbrewery, and with the help of Jack's wife, Theda, obtained the necessary permits to operate.

Rick and Jack do all the brewing themselves. They are fanatical about remaining faithful to the styles of beer they produce. Only high quality whole-leaf hops and malted brewer's grains are used. Rick smells and tastes the product at various stages to ensure that it meets his expectations.

In the beginning, all of Rikenjak's beer went into kegs. The Chimes restaurant at LSU was its first customer. Starting in January, 1994, they began bottling, and their distribution network widened to include the Lafayette and New Orleans areas.

Three varieties of Rikenjak's are currently available. *Old Hardhead Scottish Ale* is a traditional Scottish ale with a deep, dark color and a pronounced malty flavor. *Real Ale* is a British bitter similar to English pub offerings. *American Ale* is light and smooth with very little aftertaste. Plans are underway for two new products: a traditional lager, and a variation of existing recipes for sale in Mississippi (Mississippi requires lower alcohol content).

Rikenjak's turns out 65 barrels per month in its present location. However, Nyberg and Little expect to relocate to Feliciana Cellars Winery in November, 1994, where they will be able to boost production five-fold. Beer fanciers should have an easier time locating Rikenjak's there.

When you visit Feliciana Cellars (see p. 101), be sure to stop by Rikenjak's and pick up a few bottles. Or make the effort to track it down in stores. Either way, I think you'll agree the search was worth it.

Rikenjak's will be located at Feliciana Cellars Winery on La. 10 in Jackson after November, 1994. Take I-55 to exit 53 (La. 10) and drive about 35 miles west into Jackson; or take I-110 north from Baton Rouge to La. 19, La. 19 north to La. 10, then left on La. 10 about 5 miles. Call (504) 634-2785 for more information.

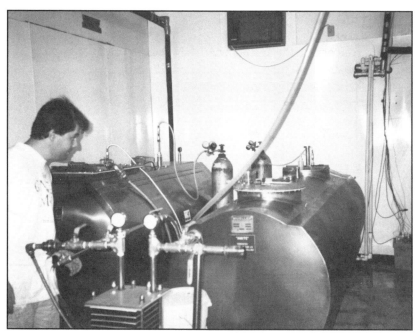

Rick Nyberg at Rikenjak's

ABITA BREWERY
Abita Springs

A tour of Abita Brewery begins, fittingly, with a beer. As inquisitive visitors drift into Abita's large, mysterious brewing and bottling plant, a guide ushers them into a tasting room to have an introductory draft—Turbo Dog, Fall Festival, Purple Haze, or whatever's new at the brewery. All eagerly accept. It's a great way to enter a frame of mind conducive to learning about the complex process of brewing. The guide carries a cup, too.

Brewing begins with a grinding machine. Grains of barley are poured into this machine (which looks a little like a coin counter) and popped open, but not pulverized. Natural spring water is filtered through the popped grains in a manner similar to drip-brewing coffee.

The filtered liquid is steeped for 1½ hours, then transferred to a kettle to boil for another 1½ hours. From there the boiled liquid goes to a whirlpool tank where Yakima Valley hops are added. Intense centrifuging causes the hops and other solids to coalesce in a column in the center of the tank, where they are easily drained out through a hole in the bottom.

The mixture is piped to fermentation tanks where it is kept at 50-60° F for approximately five days. After fermentation, the raw beer, or *wort*, is transferred to aging tanks which already contain hybrid German yeast. The yeast converts grain sugar to alcohol and gives off carbon dioxide. Fermentation and aging tanks are giant, metallic structures that look like rocket stages. The *wort* is aged five to twenty-one days at 32° F and then "cold filtered."

Finished beer is put in bottles at a rate of six cases a minute. Abita currently sells over a million bottles a year. Quality control is nonetheless very strict: pH levels, alcohol levels, and other indices are closely monitored in an on-site laboratory before the product is bottled.

Abita Brewery was founded in 1986 by Jim and Kathleen Patton. Looking at the complicated network of tanks, pipes, filters, and bottlers, it's hard to believe that neither Jim nor Kathleen has a food industry background. They're anthropologists. They brewed beer at home for a number of years, then decided to make the leap into full-time production. The operation grew as demand escalated and as they acquired industrial

Fermenting tanks at Abita Brewery

equipment from quarreling attorneys and other unlikely sources.

Amber, a lager, is Abita's most popular offering. The Pattons are highly experimental, however, and love to invent special beers. Purple Haze's surprising flavor comes from raspberry juice. Turbo Dog is a light-bodied but dark beer that debuted at Mardi Gras in New Orleans. The Pattons knew Turbo Dog would be a hit when they heard a crowd of French Quarter revelers barking at a waitress.

Abita does not pasteurize its beer. The heat of pasteurization can rob a beer of its distinctive flavor. Abita products thus have a shelf life of about sixty days. Vendors never have to worry about shelf life, because customers buy out the stock so fast.

At the end of the tour, visitors are invited back to the tasting room. The tour guide joins in. There's no limit on how much visitors can drink, though restraint should be exercised if you have to drive. An hour at Abita Brewery is delightfully informative and well worth the trip to St. Tammany Parish.

Tours are held every Saturday at 1:00 p.m. Admission free. Abita Brewery is located in Abita Springs, about 25 miles east of Hammond. Call (504) 893-3143 in the middle of the week to make reservations and obtain precise directions.

Remote Sites

WATERFALL
Catahoula Parish

OK, Niagara it's not. But in a state known for its bayous and swamps, this Catahoula Parish cascade is a refreshing change of pace.

It drops first six feet, then another fourteen feet into a shallow plunge pool. After a hard rain, the sound of splashing is audible several hundred yards away. You may be tempted to scramble down to the base of the fall, or straddle the ledge and look down (the creek's not too wide). If so, give in. Or you may just want to sit and listen.

Inconspicuously marked, this jewel has escaped the notice of all but the most inquisitive non-locals. Louisiana has incorporated it into the Sicily Island Hills Wildlife Management Area, which should give it some well-deserved exposure. If natives of nearby Harrisonburg and Sicily Island would rather keep it a secret, it's easy to see why.

To see the waterfall, take La. 15 to Sicily Island. Turn west on La. 8 at the sharp

Waterfall, Catahoula Parish

bend in the road. Follow La. 8 for about seven miles. Watch for a white brick house with a tan roof. Turn right at the gravel parking lot across from this house. You'll see three unpaved roads leading from the parking lot. Take the *middle* road (a roadmark to check for is an I-40 sign incongruously posted on a tree near the beginning) and follow it approximately 2.7 miles. At a widening of the road, you'll see a wooden sign that says "Nature Trail." Park here.

Follow the signs along a path that curves like the letter *C*. After a brief hike you'll see the waterfall (but probably hear it first). The terrain is rugged, so hiking boots are recommended.

An added attraction of this area is the "miniature Grand Canyon" visible on the right at approximately two miles from the beginning of the middle gravel road. You'll be amazed how much this one resembles its famous southwestern counterpart.

An administrative point: you must purchase a basic fishing license before entering a Wildlife Management area. Licenses are available at large discount stores and sporting goods stores for $5.00. If you're a lover of natural beauty, put on a pair of hiking boots and look for this stunning spectacle.

The Grand Canyon of Central Louisiana

UNCLE TOM'S GRAVE

Natchitoches Parish, near Chopin

Most people who venture into this area are turkey hunters. Aside from a Union Pacific Railroad track and a few muffled rumblings from 18-wheelers on the interstate over a mile away, there is no sign of human activity. In the hilly woods above an ox-bow lake that once connected with the Red River, there lie two bronze headstones surrounded by wrought iron fences. One headstone commemorates Robert McAlpin, the alleged real-life model for Simon Legree in Harriet Beecher Stowe's *Uncle Tom's Cabin*; the other commemorates the model for Uncle Tom himself.

The plots are clearly visible, but are not on a well-worn trail. No historical placard directs visitors toward them or explains their relevance. I learned of them from a Civil War relic hunter who stumbled upon them while metal detecting. The ornate fences and well-kept headstones suggest that someone has devoted considerable time and money to preserving what he or she feels is a historical legacy. But what would lead someone to think Uncle Tom and Simon Legree were buried in rural southeast Natchitoches Parish?

One theory is discussed at length by Lyle Saxon in *Old Louisiana*.[1] He chronicles a controversy that started in the 1890s

The alleged grave of uncle Tom

when Judge D. B. Corley of Abilene, Texas, purchased a cabin believed to have housed "Uncle Tom." The owner, Lammy Chopin, inherited the property from his father, who in turn had bought it from Robert McAlpin, the supposed model for Simon Legree.

Chopin's plantation bore certain similarities to the one described in *Uncle Tom's Cabin*. It was on the Red River, surrounded by hills and swamps, and it had a stand of chinaberry trees. McAlpin himself was a transplanted New England bachelor, as was Legree. McAlpin was an alcoholic who treated slaves badly according to some accounts; one of his old slaves was named Tom. Judge Corley conducted numerous oral interviews with elderly people in the vicinity, all of whom confirmed his version of the story. In Stowe's novel, Uncle Tom was buried in a "dry, sandy knoll, shaded by a few trees"[2] beyond the boundaries of the plantation; this would correlate roughly to the terrain where the present day graves lie (assuming more trees might have sprung up since the 1850s).

Saxon's presentation is balanced. He judiciously reprints a letter from a member of the Louisiana Historical Society which systematically refutes many Uncle Tom legends, including a persistent one that Harriet Beecher Stowe visited McAlpin in Louisiana. Stowe herself said in many places that Simon Legree and Uncle Tom were composite characters drawn from hundreds of subjects.

Whether these graves near Chopin contain the remains of the real Simon Legree and Uncle Tom or not, the possibility invites thought. Adventuresome travelers are encouraged to visit and draw their own conclusions.

Take I-49 to exit 113 (Chopin), which is about 25 miles north of Alexandria. Turn right at the bottom of the ramp. Almost immediately, you'll see a railroad track. Pull off the road here and park. On foot, turn right at the railroad track and follow it about ½ mile. You'll see a path leading up a hill to your left. Follow this path a few hundred feet and you'll see a wrought-iron enclosure with Uncle Tom's alleged grave. Continue down the path a short distance and you'll find a similar enclosure with Robert McAlpin's grave. The terrain is rough, so wear sturdy walking shoes or hiking boots.

[1]Lyle Saxon, *Old Louisiana*. New York: The Century Company, 1929, p. 253 - 266.
[2]Harriet Beecher Stowe, *Uncle Tom's Cabin*, Elizabeth Ammons, ed. W. W. Norton Company, New York, 1994, p. 364.

DRISKILL MOUNTAIN
Near Bienville, Bienville Parish

At 535 feet above sea level, Driskill Mountain hardly impresses most people as a mountain. Without a marker, few could distinguish it from the surrounding sparsely settled hills and forests of North Central Louisiana. Mention it to someone from Colorado and you're guaranteed to evoke laughter. Yet, it's the highest point in the Bayou State, and it's the closest you'll get to the stars without traveling many miles north. Mississippi's Woodall Mountain, at a dizzying 802 feet, looms like Mount Everest by comparison. Only two states can boast lower maximum elevations than Louisiana: Florida, with 345 feet, and Delaware, with 442 feet.

The approach to Driskill Mountain may be more adventuresome than the actual climb. Driskill Mountain is located in northeast Bienville Parish, nine miles due south of Arcadia and approximately halfway between Monroe and Shreveport. Travelers from South Louisiana should start by going to Alexandria. Pick up U.S. 167 in Alexandria and ride it about 84 miles northward to Hodge, where you fork to the left on La. 147 and follow it to the juncture with La. 507. Turn west (left) at La. 507. In just a mile or two, you should see Mt. Zion Presbyterian Church on the right. A sign in front of the church marks the mountain trailhead.

Travelers in North Louisiana should take I-20 to Arcadia (La. 9) and go south. Veer left onto La. 147 where La. 9 and La. 147 diverge. Follow La. 147 to La. 507 and turn west (right). Look for Mt. Zion Presbyterian Church on the right.

It's up to you whether you want to walk or drive the trail. A pickup or four-wheel-drive vehicle is recommended for driving. I made it in a small Toyota, but scraped bottom

several times. Driving is probably not a good idea in wet weather. If you walk, wear hiking boots and insect repellent. Snakes have been reported in the area.

The trail beginning at the left side of Mt. Zion Church leads all the way to the "peak" of the mountain. The maximum elevation point is marked by a small sign.

Driskill Mountain has become a popular spot for families to picnic and for couples to...well, be couples. It may not be a purist's mountain, but it's *our* mountain, so you owe it to yourself to scale its vertiginous slopes at least once.

Driskill Mountain's peak

BONNIE & CLYDE AMBUSH SITE

Gibsland

Pock-marked, scratched, and illegible in places, this gravestone-like concrete monument on La. 154 south of Gibsland hardly seems equal to the horrific event it commemorates. On May 23, 1934, two of the most vicious criminals in American history were ambushed here by a posse of special agents. Bonnie Parker and Clyde Barrow took so many shots that morticians later complained their bodies wouldn't retain embalming fluids.

Such a concentrated assault was needed because Bonnie and Clyde weren't fond of surrender. They routinely eluded police chases, slipped through dragnets, took hostages, and killed policemen. All the while, they cut a swath of crime through the Midwest that captured worldwide headlines and earned them the #1 position on the FBI's most wanted list.

Clyde Barrow was born dirt poor. He began to exhibit antisocial behavior from a very early age. He had already been jailed once and committed several small-time robberies by the time he met Bonnie Parker in 1930. Bonnie was waitressing in a café while her estranged husband served a 99-year sentence for murder. She joined Clyde for excitement.

Between 1930 and 1934, Bonnie and Clyde and their gang (which frequently included Clyde's brother Buck and wife Blanche) are known to have committed a dozen murders and nearly as many

Bonnie and Clyde marker

robberies. The largest heist they ever made was $1,500. Their targets were gas stations, liquor stores, small town banks, and restaurants. Their victims were ordinary folk who were trying to eke out a living during the Great Depression. Although Bonnie and Clyde achieved folk hero status posthumously, they were despised during their lives by small-town dwellers in the Midwest who constituted their prey. Robbery and murder were mere recreation for Bonnie and Clyde.

Clyde served 20 months at Eastham Prison Farm in eastern Texas for a bank robbery. During those months, he bludgeoned his cellmate to death with a lead pipe and became converted to homosexuality. After his inexplicable parole, he reestablished contact with Bonnie. On one of their jaunts, they took a hostage, W. D. Jones, a gas station attendant who was looking for kicks. Jones was forced to shoot people and have sex with both Clyde and Bonnie.

Bonnie and Clyde were not Robin Hoods; they were re-morseless sociopaths who could have carried on their career of mayhem indefinitely had not one of their former associates told federal agents where to trap them. After the ambush, Bonnie and Clyde's bullet-riddled tan V-8 Ford was towed through the streets of Arcadia as an example to the children that crime doesn't pay.

Standing in front of the Bonnie and Clyde monument on La. 154, it's difficult not to get a *frisson* of excitement from the thought that two of America's most notorious villains met their doom on this spot. But the excitement is quickly succeeded by relief. Perhaps the bullet holes in the concrete reflect how history will ultimately regard Bonnie and Clyde.

To view the Bonnie and Clyde marker, exit I-20 at La. 154 (about 39 miles east of Shreveport). Stay on La. 154 (turn to follow it) for about 8 miles. A sign will advise you of the marker about 1 mile in advance.

A festival honoring Bonnie and Clyde has recently been started in Arcadia. It will be held on the weekend nearest May 23rd and will feature a re-enactment of the 1934 ambush. For more information, call (318) 263-9897.

Sources: Hinton, Ted. *Ambush: The Real Story of Bonnie and Clyde*. Bryan, Texas: Shoal Creek Publishers, Inc., 1979. Nash, Jay. *Bloodletters and Badmen*. New York: M. Evans and Company, Inc., 1973.

Lagniappe

TRADER'S RENDEZVOUS FRONTIER VILLAGE
Bentley

Some people collect antique dolls or clocks. Alton Thorne collects antique *houses*. He's been hauling them in from all over Grant and LaSalle Parishes for more than a decade, and now he has enough to make up a flourishing village—of an earlier era, that is.

Mr. Thorne has relocated literally dozens of late nineteenth century and early twentieth century buildings to his facility in Bentley. He's restored them enough to ensure their structural integrity, but not so much as to mask the sturdy craftsmanship that enabled them to stand so long. The buildings are arranged around a town square, with a schoolhouse, jailhouse, barbershop, blacksmith shop, and newspaper office. There's even a privy (with corncobs and a Sears catalog provided)!

Trader's Rendezvous Frontier Village is no mere ghost town. It is a *working community* where the old ways of the turn of the century come to life. Villagers in period costume make lye soap, press sugar cane, saw wood, smoke bacon, and even distill whiskey using authentic equipment. Visitors can draw water from a functioning deep well pitcher pump.

Mr. Thorne, at one time a diecaster who built tools for a farm equipment company, has found and reconditioned all the machinery at the Frontier Village. Everything *works*. Steam engines, band saws, drill presses, gristmills, haybalers, thrashing machines, you name it. "This is not a 'no touch place,'" he emphasizes. "You can see, smell, hear, taste, and feel things the way they really were."

Don't miss the 80-foot fire tower. Used for many years by the Forestry Service, it was so large that Mr. Thorne had to dismantle it into three sections to transport it. Now it gives an excellent prospect of the Frontier Village and most of Grant Parish.

To go to Trader's Rendezvous Frontier Village, take La. 167 north from Alexandria until you get to La. 8. Take a right (east) onto La. 8, and the facility will be immediately on your left. The complete tour takes about 1½ hours. Admission charged. There's also a gift shop and restaurant. For more information, call (318) 899-5454.

"One-lunger" generator

FRENCH QUARTER AUTHORS TOUR

New Orleans

New Orleans gave us the words *cocktail* and *Dixie*. If it made no further contribution to American letters, its place in literary history would be assured. But it gave us ever so much more. Authors as diverse as Sherwood Anderson, William Faulkner, and Lafcadio Hearn lived there, took inspiration from its exotic sights and sounds, and produced some of their finest works there. For an introduction to this often overlooked literary aspect of Crescent City history, take a walking tour of the French Quarter with Kenneth Holditch, Ph.D., or one of his associates.

See the apartment where Tennessee Williams sat writing when his concentration was broken by a streetcar named Desire. See

One of Tennessee Williams's former apartments

the apartments he rented during his so-called "stoned age."

Walk past the glorious Monteleone Hotel, where Truman Capote's father once spent six months *gratis* thanks to Capote's renown and influence.

Take a long look at the elegant restaurant where William Faulkner spent all the advance money for his first novel, *Mosquitoes*, on one grand luncheon. See the café table under which Anita Luce first spied a besotted Faulkner sleeping. Gaze at the tiny room where Faulkner played devious pranks on passersby with one of his friends.

Hear the intriguing story of the Old Absinthe House, a French Quarter pub whose illustrious guests have included William Makepeace Thackeray, Oscar Wilde, O'Henry, Mark Twain, Walt Whitman, and others.

Duck into the narrow alley where Beat Generation guru William S. Burroughs bought heroin in his pre-*Naked Lunch* days.

See the old D. H. Holmes building immortalized in John Kennedy Toole's *Confederacy of Dunces.* Hear for the first time the true story of how that Pulitzer Prize-winning novel came to be published.

Walk the streets haunted by Lafcadio Hearn as he sought disconsolately to immerse himself in the city's myriad ethnic groups.

Learn how Storyville, America's only legalized red light district, was instituted, allowed to flourish, and dismantled. Learn how disparate cultural and musical streams converged in a New Orleans park to form jazz. Learn how New Orleans evolved from an outpost to a thriving port and finally a literary mecca... and much, much more about this intriguing American city.

Kenneth Holditch holds a Ph.D. from the University of Mississippi and teaches at the University of New Orleans. He and his associates conduct walking tours of the French Quarter designed not only to show where literary figures once lived, but to illustrate how the spirit of New Orleans has served as a muse for generations of writers. Along the way, they provide many insights into the social and cultural milieu in which these writers operated. Questions are welcomed.

This tour takes about two hours and could easily be substituted for a more conventional tour. The cost is competitive with other tours in the French Quarter. Call (504) 949-9805 for information and reservations.

EVANGELINE OAK

St. Martinville

No visit to Acadiana would be complete without a moment of silence before the Evangeline Oak in St. Martinville. Legend has it that Emmeline Labiche and Louis Arceneaux, two lovers forced apart by the British during the expulsion of the Acadians from Nova Scotia in 1755, had a fateful rendezvous under this tree many years later.

New England poet Henry Wadsworth Longfellow gave the couple immortality in his 1847 epic, *Evangeline*. In Longfellow's version of the story, Evangeline Bellefontaine (Emmeline Labiche) and Gabriel Lajeunesse (Louis Arceneaux) are driven into exile the day after their engagement party. Heartsick Evangeline rides a boat down the Mississippi in search of Gabriel, but just misses him at his father's farm. She trails Gabriel all over the country, always arriving too late; she begins to think she's tracking a ghost. At one point she weeps under a large oak tree.

Evangeline Oak

Years later, as a Sister of Mercy in Philadelphia, she happens upon Gabriel in a poorhouse, plague-stricken and near death. He dies, and she dies shortly thereafter.

Louisiana writer Felix Voorhies recorded the story in a 1907 prose volume, *Acadian Reminiscences.* His account parallels Longfellow's in certain points but diverges from it in others. According to Voorhies, Emmeline witnesses Louis being viciously beaten by British soldiers and for a time fears he's dead. Emmeline is sent to Maryland, Louis to Louisiana. Emmeline makes a long pilgrimage to Louisiana, where she finds Louis reclining under a large oak beside the Teche River. He glumly informs her that he's married another woman and that she should forget him. Emmeline is devastated; she suffers a nervous breakdown and spends the rest of her life in a daze, wandering the banks of the Teche, picking flowers and singing Acadian songs. She dies of a broken heart.

In view of the worldwide recognition brought to the Acadian plight by *Evangeline*, Longfellow can be forgiven for elaborating on the basic story somewhat. But Voorhies' version is not above question; *Acadian Reminiscences* appeared sixty years after *Evangeline* and displays a similarly romantic style.

Whichever version you accept, you'll find that the Evangeline Oak has an unmistakable aura. Its trunk is wide and ancient; its gnarled branches give it a mournful demeanor that seems to bear out the legends associated with it. Behind the tree is a boardwalk overlooking the Teche and a pavilion. Cajuns sit on benches conversing in French and exhorting tourists to take pictures of the French side of the historical marker. When you visit Evangeline Oak, you participate in an experience very near the heart of Cajun culture.

To see Evangeline Oak, take U.S. 90 south from Lafayette to Broussard. Turn left on La. 96 in Broussard. Follow La. 96 about seven miles to St. Martinville. Turn right just before Bayou Teche. Evangeline Oak is about a block down on the left. For information on St. Martinville, call (318) 394-2233.

MODEL AGE PROGRESSION LABORATORY

Baton Rouge

Finding a missing child gets more difficult the longer he is missing, because a child's features can change dramatically as he grows and develops, often to the extent that his own parents are not able to recognize him.

Law enforcement agencies increasingly rely on *age progression* for help in solving missing child cases. *Age progression* is a subdiscipline of forensic anthropology that involves compiling known physiological information about a missing child, correlating it to nationwide growth statistics, and constructing visual images of what the child might look like at various stages of development. Analysts use computer programs and clay facial modeling to make projections for police.

Louisiana is fortunate to have one of only six age progression laboratories in the United States, and the only such laboratory based at a university. Mary Manhein, an instructor in LSU's Department of Anthropology, led a campaign to have her depart-

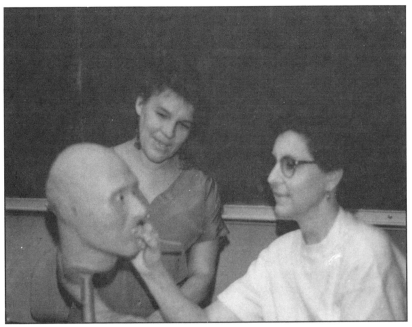

Mary Manhein and Eileen Barrow preparing a clay facial reconstruction

ment designated a Model Age Progression Laboratory several years ago. Today, the laboratory is linked with the National Center for Missing and Exploited Children and collaborates with law enforcement agencies all over the country. Manhein's expertise has been tapped by the Fox network series, *Missing*.

By spring 1995, a one-of-a-kind public education center will open in the former Museum of Geoscience on the LSU campus in Baton Rouge. This center will offer demonstrations of computer-aided age progression and clay facial reconstruction, and will provide information on how to prevent children from being abducted. Admission will be free. Guides will be on hand to explain age progression techniques and answer questions.

Dynamic Mary Manhein divides her time between the Model Age Progression Laboratory and her duties as Deputy Coroner of East Baton Rouge Parish. Whenever human remains are found, she's called in to make a determination of the time and cause of death. Much of her time is spent excavating old burial sites. Highway crews recently uncovered a 19th-century burial ground for medical school cadavers, and Manhein was contacted. The literally hundreds of skeletons retrieved at the site told a chilling tale about how medicine was taught and practiced in the 19th century. Manhein and her able assistant, Eileen Barrow, were major consultants at the 1993 exhumation of Dr. Carl Weiss, alleged assassin of Huey Long. Both are in frequent contact with Dr. Douglas Ubelaker, curator of natural anthropology at the National Museum of Natural History at the Smithsonian Institution and co-author of the nationwide best-seller, *Bones: A Forensic Detective's Casebook*.

Though grounded in rigorous deductive techniques, forensic anthropology requires intuition, an ability to fill in gaps between facts, and peer into the dark side of human nature. Manhein, whose first degree was in creative writing, finds this aspect of the subject deeply rewarding. But what pleases her most is closing a case, giving an anguished parent the solace of knowing exactly where his or her child is.

The Model Age Progression public information center will be located in front of the Howe-Russell Geoscience Complex at LSU in Baton Rouge, and should be open to the public by Spring, 1995. For more information, call (504) 388-6084.

STATUE OF BUDDHA
Avery Island

South Louisiana is overwhelmingly Roman Catholic. The influence of Catholicism is easy to detect, especially in smaller towns: concrete Virgin Mary grottoes grace many a front lawn; highway billboards advertise mass schedules instead of hotel rates; church buildings dominate skylines. Visitors to Avery Island in coastal Iberia Parish can thus be forgiven for wondering why a larger-than-life statue of Buddha gazes out over a swamp at the rear of the Jungle Gardens.

The statue came into Edward Avery McIlhenny's hands through an improbable chain of events. During the final days of the Ch'ing Dynasty (1644 A.D. to 1912 A.D.), a Chinese general purloined the statue from Shonfa Temple near Beijing. It was an ancient statue, dating from the Sung Dynasty (960 A.D. to 1279 A.D.), and the general hoped to sell it to a museum in New York. Unfortunately, he was captured and beheaded by the Chinese army before the deal went through. Friends of McIlhenny procured the statue and had it shipped to Avery Island.

McIlhenny (son of the founder of the Tabasco empire) was no mere dabbler in exotic imports. He was a world traveler with a sophisticated understanding of natural science, folklore, and foreign languages. He wrote numerous books and received visitors from all parts of the world.

One of his most celebrated achievements was the preservation of the snowy egret. Egret feathers were in great demand as adornment for women's hats in the late nineteenth century, and the egret was nearly hunted to extinction. McIlhenny captured seven baby egrets and constructed huge bamboo "flying cages" for them. He fed, nurtured, and protected them, then released them to the wild when they were grown. They flew away, but returned to the same spot the next year to bear their young. Egrets now flock to the same lake, "Bird City" as it is now called, by the thousands.

The flying cages are gone, but an international ambience remains. Trees from England, France, China, Japan, and Africa flourish in Avery Island's distinctively South Louisiana setting. McIlhenny had a great appreciation for other cultures and systems of faith, and the statue of Buddha can be viewed as a manifesta-

Pagoda at Avery Island

tion of that appreciation. The bamboo woods and serene swamp surrounding the pagoda make Buddha seem quite at home.

The Jungle Gardens of Avery Island are luxuriant, graceful, and quiet. You can spend many hours on the pathways taking photographs and harmonizing with nature. While you're on Avery Island, you can also tour the McIlhenny Plantation and the Tabasco Plant. Avery Island, incidentally, is a geological oddity in that it rests on a giant salt dome, which lifts it to an elevation of 155 feet above sea level.

Statue of Buddha

To get to Avery Island, take U.S. 90 south from Lafayette to La. 329. Turn right. Signs will direct you to the McIlhenny Plantation. A modest admission is charged. For more information, call (318) 369-6243.

INDEX

Keith Odom is a native Louisianian
who was raised in Baton Rouge, and
graduated from Louisiana State
University. Keith likes to read, write,
and travel. He has visited various
parts of the United States and
Europe, and has lived and taught
school in Japan. He enjoys meeting
people of diverse cultures and learning about their ways of life. He has a
large, laid-back tabby cat who kept
him company through the writing of
Only in Louisiana.

OTHER BOOKS OF RELATED INTEREST:

Only in Mississippi
ISBN 0-937552-54-2, 96 pages, paperbound, $5.95

A History Lover's Guide to Louisiana
ISBN 0-937552-37-2, 240 pages, paperbound, $12.95